It's Now or Never –

The Seven Key Strategies to Wealth Creation for Employees

What People
Are Saying about This Book

"Although there are many professional and highly qualified employees, when it comes to personal wealth planning, they are either ignorant or clueless. This book creates awareness among readers of the importance of early personal wealth planning, and it offers practical methods to create wealth. The author is a successful professional and business coach who has plenty of realistic wealth accumulation experience to share with us. Overall, I find this book interesting, informative, motivating, and useful."

—Dr. Venus Khim-Sen Liew
Associate Professor of Economics and Business
University Malaysia Sarawak

"The book is beautifully written. The strategies used are very practical for everyone. The concept of wealth is explained well. Readers will certainly get the maximum benefit from the book when they apply the recommended strategies. I would like to thank the author for sharing his failures and successes in different chapters; they reinforce the idea that all employees can be wealthy if they sincerely believe in themselves, work hard, and follow a proven system. This book will definitely help readers change their views and perceptions regarding spending, saving, and investing. Read this book, and start building personal wealth."

—Manohar Rao Shivaji Shinde
PD&E Analyst
Saudi Aramco

"As someone from a decidedly non-financial background, I find Dr. Frank Kiong's book a remarkably clear and easy-to-follow guide to the simple strategies for increasing financial health. One doesn't need a PhD in finance or years of experience in the stock markets to gain wealth—just read this book! It is packed with practical ideas, home truths, and concrete advice for anyone who wonders where all the dollars and cents disappear to at the end of the month and how to can get them back!"

—Dr. Simon Botley @ Faizal Hakim
Associate Professor of English Language
Universiti Teknologi MARA Sarawak

Also by Dr. Frank Kiong

Dare to Change:
A Step-by-Step Guide for Top Achievers

Peeling Your Onion:
The Magic to Your True Potential

It's Now or Never –
The Seven Key Strategies to Wealth Creation for Employees

How to Become Rich Without Quitting Your Day Job!

Dr. Frank Kiong

PARTRIDGE

To order additional copies of this book, contact
Toll Free 800 101 2657 (Singapore)
Toll Free 1 800 81 7340 (Malaysia)
orders.singapore@partridgepublishing.com

www.partridgepublishing.com/singapore

This book is dedicated to employees like you who want to create wealth but can't see a way of doing so.

The strategies presented in this book are not new and have been adopted by many people, even during Babylonian times. These strategies can help employees and indeed anyone to create wealth that will last for years.

Use these strategies not only to accumulate wealth and get out of debt systematically and quickly, but more importantly, to end your money worries for good. My advice is this: don't take my word literally; implement these strategies yourselves to see positive results.

Contents

Acknowledgments

I would like to express my gratitude to the many people who helped me create this book, to all those who provided support, read it, reviewed it, offered comments, and assisted in the editing, proofreading, and design.

I would like to thank my wife, Paula, and my four children, Kimberleey, Beverly, Richie, and Keith. We began this journey together, and you all sink and swim with me through bad times and good times. Thank you for supporting me and encouraging me to write and publish this book in spite of all the times it took me away from you all.

To my dad and mom, my brothers, and my sisters: many thanks for your support throughout the years.

To Associate Professor Dr. Simon Faizal Hakim, Associate Professor Dr. Venus Khim-Sen Liew, George Sikien Sunow, Manohar Rao Shivaji Shinde, and Wade Rand, thank you for helping me to review the manuscript and for offering comments and suggestions. All of you are extraordinary!

To Edmundo Rodriguez, thank you for the great pieces of art that are included in this book. You are the most talented artist I have ever associated with.

To my publishing consultants, Dianne Marie and Sydney Felicio, and the staff from Partridge Publishing, thank you so much, because without your guidance and support, this book would never find its way to the bookstores or the Web.

I beg forgiveness of all those who have been supporting me over the years whose names I have failed to mention.

And finally, thanks to you, the readers, for being willing to buy this book and follow the strategies and advice in its pages. I truly believe that nothing is impossible when you have found the real purpose of your life. So be the best you can be, because indeed you are unstoppable!

Introduction

It's now or never!
This is the right time for you to get out of debt, create your wealth, and live the life you truly deserve.

I remember the darkest day of my life: Christmas Eve 2007. Normally on that special day, Christians are busy preparing for Christmas; however, I was busy battling and avoiding the banks, as they were continually calling and demanding that I pay my three months of outstanding mortgage and car loans.

A week before, I had received a letter from the bank reminding me that one of my cars would be repossessed if I failed to make at least a one-month payment. To further inflict injury to my already serious financial problems, another bank was calling, demanding that I pay my credit card bill, which had been outstanding for several months. Honestly, I was buried in a mountain of debt.

The whole ordeal with the banks ruined our Christmas preparations. I told my wife that we should cancel our Christmas celebration because we were so financially tight—I was late on all my loan payments.

My children failed to understand why we didn't buy anything for that Christmas. I could understand why. They were too young to understand our financial problems, and they had been looking forward to the celebration. Who wouldn't at that age?

On Christmas Day itself, my youngest son at that time asked, "Daddy, why didn't you buy any presents?" I was speechless. I looked at my wife, and she was speechless too. After about five minutes, she responded, "Junior, Christmas is not all about having presents; it's about having all our family members together, even over a simple dinner." I looked at my son's face, and I saw disappointment and sorrow. My heart grew heavy with sadness. But how could we expect a five-year-old to understand?

To make a long story short, I was buried under a mountain of debt because of the many bad financial decisions that I had made for a number of years. In fact, most, if not all, of the bad financial decisions were based on fulfilling my ego and my desires. Although I had a good Mitsubishi Pajero, I had thought it would be cool to have a BMW because I was an associate professor and the head of a university in my state. I also thought it would be cool to buy expensive clothes and shoes, since I was the head of a university. Although I didn't have cash to buy all those unnecessary things, I still bought them—and charged them on my credit card. After constantly charging my credit card and not paying my loans on time, I reached a critical moment in my life: I was falling deeper into debt. I was spending more than I earned, and nothing was left for savings or investment.

As I sat alone in my study one evening, lost in thought over my financial worries, my eldest daughter knocked on the door. She approached me and asked, "Daddy, are we rich?" I didn't answer her question; in fact, I was dumbfounded by it.

I asked, "How was your day at school?"

She looked at me and said, "I don't like going to Chinese school."

"Why?"

"The teachers are very strict, and I am scared." She then left my study.

After my daughter left, I thought about her question. I felt bad not answering her and being truthful to her, but I felt it was better to keep the answer to myself.

That night I couldn't sleep; I kept thinking about my daughter's question. Then the answer gushed out of my mind: "Frank, you are not wealthy but you pretend to be. You are kidding yourself!" Oh my goodness, I felt as if someone had just slapped me very hard on the face, literally waking me up.

The thought of pretending to be wealthy when I was not made me feel really bad. The two nice cars and two classic cars that I had acquired a few years before had driven me onto a fast lane of debt and financial trouble. How could I, as a finance graduate, be so careless in my financial planning?

Because of my poor judgment, ego, and desires, I had burdened my family and me with a mountain of debt. But who would believe me if I told my friends that I was having financial problems when they saw my sporty black BMW and our nice house? Besides, I was the head of a university and was an associate professor with a specialization in finance. But the reality was that I was buried in debt, and I couldn't seem to get out of it.

These serious financial problems adversely affected my health. Quite honestly, a couple of times I thought of ending my life. The only reason I didn't was because of my wife and my young children. I felt that the whole world was against me. I couldn't seem to find the solutions to my financial problems. I kept the problems to myself, and I was ashamed to share them even with my close friends. The only people who knew I was in serious trouble were my wife and the banks. But rather than seek counseling from the relevant authority, I preferred to continue to live according to my pride and ego.

While driving back from the office one evening, I made a decision to change my life once and for all. But the question that kept lingering in my mind was, *How I am going to do that?* I had tried to change before. In fact, I had read many self-help books that talked about how to be successful, how to get out of debt, how to create wealth, how to think big, how to think positive, etc.

I read many books by many best-selling authors, such as Robert Kiyosaki, Dr. David Schwartz, Tom Peters, and Napoleon Hill. I am not saying that these books were bad; they were best-sellers, after all. But the more I read, the more confused I became, as each book seemed to offer different advice. In fact, toward the end of 2008, my study looked more like a library of hundreds of self-help books. Unfortunately, I was further sucked into debt.

Fast-forward a year. To get myself out of debt, I started a business with a friend. Unfortunately, our business was not successful, and I got myself deeper into debt. In creating the business, I learned many important lessons. Some were good, some were bad, and some were painful.

But the turning point that got me out of debt and into creating wealth was when my wife gave me a book. I had stopped reading self-help books, as none of them had helped me to get out of my financial troubles. So the only reason I read the book was because my wife couldn't understand the language used in it. At that time, she was doing an assignment for her bachelor's in business administration, and she happened to buy the book as one of her references. Because the language was very classical, I had to read it a couple of times to understand it. When I finished, I said to myself, *Wow, this book's ideas on money really make sense.*

Indeed, after reading the book, I set up a personal savings and investment plan for the first time and made this my priority for a couple of years. I began to focus my efforts on each of the strategies and applied the rule that I always believed in: the rule of PHD, which stands for *planning* with persistence, working *hard* on my plan, and being *disciplined* and determined to succeed. In 2010, I felt I was alive again, and by the end of 2010, I had the energy and money to publish my first motivational book, *Dare to Change.*

Within a year of working on my plan and applying the strategies outlined in the book, my cash flow became positive. And as I kept to my savings and investment plan, within two years I started to accumulate assets, and my savings increased massively. Over the next three years, my cash flow grew several fold, and by the end of the fourth year, I had accumulated substantial assets. I couldn't believe my achievement, and I was thrilled.

What was the secret that enabled me to clear all my bad debts and at the same time be able to accumulate assets quickly? My answer is simple: there is no secret. The only solution was to admit my past mistakes and make sure I strictly followed the seven strategies I will share with you in this book. These strategies indeed became my GPS to achieving financial success.

Now, if you are an employee like me, here are my questions to you:

- Do you really want to be wealthy?
- Do you find yourself clueless about how to create wealth?
- Do you find yourself trapped in a cycle of debt and don't know how to get out of it?
- Do you want to end your money worries for good?

If your answer to these questions is *yes*, this book is for you. *It's Now or Never: The Seven Key Strategies to Wealth Creation for Employees* will show you

- how to build your wealth with as little as 10 percent of your monthly salary;
- how to control your spending without depriving yourself;
- how to invest to multiply your wealth;
- how to get out of debt systematically and fast;
- how to protect your wealth (and whom you must protect your wealth from);
- how to insure your future income to last for years; and
- how to increase your ability to earn more so that you can create wealth fast and end your money worries for good.

Based on my years of hands-on experience in wealth creation and my numerous trials and errors in building wealth, this book has evolved to give you tried and tested, easy-to-follow strategies so that you can accumulate wealth that lasts for *years*.

Each chapter gives short, no-nonsense how-to answers to your questions regarding how to build substantial wealth, control your spending, systematically and effectively manage your debts, and invest successfully. Additional chapters will show you why having a wealth blueprint is important and why investing is the sure way to build wealth.

Given the right strategies and with a strong belief, positive attitude and mind-set, discipline, and patience, you will be able to create wealth and even become a millionaire. The best news of all is you will finally end your money worries for good.

Last but not least, I would like to thank you for joining this wealth creation journey. I am sure you will find it worth doing and you will definitely see a positive impact on your life. So turn the page and let the magic begin, because the time is *now*.

Chapter 1
Money and Freedom

When you have money, think of the time when you had none.
Japanese Proverb

Almost everyone wants to be wealthy. Regardless of who they are or what they do, individuals dream of becoming rich. Being wealthy is not only about having money in the bank, but also about the freedom that comes along with it.

Can you imagine how you would feel if you still had plenty of cash available in the bank after you paid all your bills each month? How would you feel being able to send your children to the best private school or college because you had the money to do so? How would you feel if you settled all your debts and the bank or debt collection agencies stopped harassing you? How would you feel if you made all your purchases with cash rather than credit? How would you feel knowing that your money worked hard for you and brought in cash every month without you even lifting a finger?

**How would you feel, knowing that your
money worked hard for you?**

1

Wealthy people feel great about the freedom money brings. They love it, and they feel they are not servants to money but vice versa. But most people are not wealthy, so they don't understand how good the feeling is. And they will constantly be servants to money. Money rules and controls them rather than them taking control and ruling over money.

Almost all people want the freedom money can bring. And everyone can have that freedom, because money never discriminates against anyone, regardless of who they are. Unfortunately, not many people know how to claim their right to that freedom. Those who know how enjoy life. Those who don't worry constantly, and they even say that money is the root of all evil to justify why they shouldn't work hard to create wealth. They stick to that belief, and they remain poor. They even convince themselves that they are not destined to be wealthy. They believe it is their fate to remain poor. Many of my friends have this mind-set, and they constantly complain about not having enough money. Unfortunately, they do nothing to change their financial health.

What Is Your Goal?

If your goal is to create wealth because you want the freedom that comes with it or you want the best for your children or you want to be free from debt or you want it for some other reason, it is vital that you do more than just talk about it: you need to take action.

In your quest to create your wealth, here are three questions you should be asking yourself:

- Do I know what I should do?
- Do I know what steps I should take to claim my financial freedom?
- Do I know what strategies I should adopt?

If you don't have answers to these questions, don't worry. This situation calls for seven key strategies to wealth creation, especially for you as an employee. You need to understand that wealth creation doesn't happen accidently. You need to execute specific strategies. This requires your PHD: not an ordinary doctor of philosophy degree, but a degree of *planning, hard work, and determination*. Most important of all, take action. But before I show you the seven key strategies, let's understand the meanings of *income* and *wealth*.

Income and Wealth

Many people think that *income* and *wealth* are the same. They are not, and we should not confuse them. Let's start with their definitions.

What is *income*? Income is the flow of cash someone receives from work in terms of wages or salary. For example, if you are an engineer or medical doctor, you need to put in long hours after years of training to get a wage or salary at the end of the month. If you stop working or get fired, the flow of cash stops, and you could find yourself in financial trouble.

Wealth is different from income because even if you stopped working right now, cash would still be coming in. So, what is wealth? In economics, wealth is defined as the net worth of a person (the value of all assets you own minus liabilities). For example, if you have real estate that you rent out or a portfolio of private businesses that you own or you have invested in shares, bonds, mutual funds, unit trusts, or other cash generators, these will bring in cash despite you not working. With this cash flow, you can maintain your lifestyle even if your employer fires you or, better still, you fire your employer. But don't do that yet!

The Goal of This Book

I honestly believe that even as employees, you and I can be wealthy. And the good news is that building your wealth doesn't require extraordinary income or your own business. All you need is a proven system or formula that you can follow. The goal of this book is to provide you with that system.

This system is the seven key strategies to wealth creation. These are tried and tested and have been applied successfully by many people, even the people of ancient Babylon.

Five years ago, I discovered these strategies and put them into action, and I was thrilled with the outcomes. Because of my positive experience, I decided to write this book to share these strategies so that you can also be wealthy. But be warned: accumulating wealth and becoming financially independent takes time. In my experience, wealth creation is akin to taking good care of your small children and watching them grow to become wise and healthy. This process is slow but sure.

The seven key strategies are not quick fixes that will make you a millionaire overnight. But if your main goal is to become financially independent over a period of time, these strategies are something you should commit to because you *have* to, not just because you *want* to.

Building wealth requires certain strategies, but you also need certain attributes. These attributes are:

- a strong belief in yourself
- a positive attitude
- a positive mind-set
- commitment
- sacrifice
- specific planning
- hard work
- determination
- vision

When you strategically implement the seven key strategies and support them rigorously with all the powerful attributes above, you will achieve financial freedom (see diagram on page 5). The seven key strategies to wealth creation are explained in detail in the remaining chapters of this book.

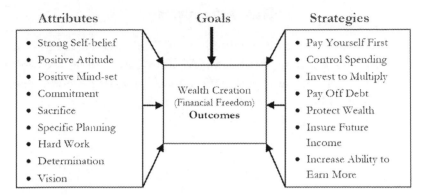

Key Takeaways

Think about the things you will take away from chapter 1 and how and when you will implement them. As an example, under the topic "Your Goal," the takeaway is "I want to have financial freedom," and for implementation you need to indicate when you will start working on this goal and when you expect to achieve it.

Topic	Takeaways	Implementation
Your Goal	I want to have financial freedom.	
What is Income?		
What is Wealth?		
Attributes for Success?		

Chapter 2
Why You Are Not Rich

You must learn to save first and spend afterwards.
H. John Poole

"Why am I not rich compared to my next-door neighbor, who is just an ordinary worker?" How many times during your career have you asked yourself this question? Or perhaps you simply ignored this question, saying that you are just not as lucky as your next-door neighbor. But let me tell you, luck will never favor anyone who doesn't take action to improve himself or herself. This chapter discusses the following:

- belief
- attitude
- mind-set
- the importance of turning negative experience into positive
- the importance of a Personal Life Plan (PLP)

Did you know that there are at least five things all successful people have in common?

- They have a dream.
- They have a plan.
- They have specific knowledge and training.
- They don't take no for an answer.
- They take action and are willing to work hard to achieve their goals.

Successful people understand that when they have embraced the first four factors and put them into action, they can make a difference in their own lives and in the lives of others.

7

Many people talk about taking action, but few do it. Some people are extremely good at talking but really awful when it is time to take action. You can find this type of person all over the world and throughout all organizations.

Research shows that an unwillingness to take action is based on three factors: *belief, attitude,* and *mind-set*. I call this the BAM triangle (see diagram below). This triangle consists of three factors that prevent many people from being free and choosing their own paths. As a result, they are poor and live in mediocrity.

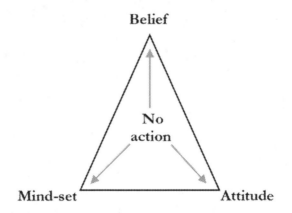

The first factor in the BAM triangle is belief. Belief is closely associated with the way social conditioning holds us back. From earliest childhood, we are trained to fit in, to play by the rules. Individuality is generally discouraged. Phrases like "don't rock the boat" and "don't make waves" imply that we should keep the status quo at all costs. Whether or not we consciously accept the truth of these beliefs, they become ingrained in our subconscious mind, and they are very difficult to get rid of. Many people bring them to their grave rather than try to change them.

Actually, belief is not so bad if you are able to switch it from negative to positive. Having positive beliefs provides fuel for the perseverance you need to succeed. Once you cultivate positive beliefs in your mind, you can achieve anything you set your mind to. Trust me on this.

Since I left America in 1994 after my finance professor told me I was not going to be successful in completing a PhD study, I worked very hard to get myself to believe I could be successful. I was very determined; I endlessly told myself I was going to be successful, and I eventually proved my finance professor wrong. I not only completed my PhD in less than three years, I passed with flying colors. Since then I have achieved many of the goals I set, both in my professional career and in the financial aspects of my life.

With strong and positive belief deeply embedded in our thoughts, all of us are indeed unstoppable; all of us can be successful in our career or in any endeavor we choose to pursue. You must believe that you can be wealthy, even if you are just an ordinary employee. Once you have a strong and positive belief, nothing can stop you. Trust me!

In fact, the only person who can deny you success is you. Remember this African proverb: "When there is no enemy within, the enemies outside cannot hurt you." Hence, don't even think of creating an enemy inside—instead, create and nurture the warrior inside.

The second factor is negative attitude. Studies show that a negative attitude can seriously hinder your progress. But think of attitude as a two-sided coin. On one side of the coin, attitude can be optimistic; on the other side, it can be pessimistic. When you are optimistic and anticipate successful encounters, you transmit a positive attitude, and people usually respond favorably. When you are pessimistic, expecting the worst, your attitude is negative, and people tend to avoid you. Think of your attitude as your mental focus on the outside world. Just as you can focus on something with a camera, you can use your mind to focus on what appeals to you. You can see situations either as opportunities or as failures. When you are facing life's biggest challenges, you see them either as opportunities to do your best and overcome the challenges, or as barriers, and you feel sorry for yourself. The choice is yours.

Attitude is not something you inherited from your parents. And none of us was born with attitudes. Our attitudes are developed as we grow. Most are shaped during our formative years. Since your attitudes are something you developed, you can change them. Don't allow negative attitudes to stop you from reaching your financial goals.

When you cultivate positive attitudes, you realize that you are walking on acres and acres of diamonds—right under your feet. But you won't be able to recognize them if your attitude is negative. If people give you a diamond, you will not appreciate it, because you will think it's just another stone. So many of us are given diamonds throughout our career, but not many convert them into wealth, due to our negative attitudes and perceptions.

Every time I changed my job or moved to another organization, I saw acres and acres of diamonds, and I made sure I harvested those diamonds (in terms of financial rewards, work experiences, and networking). Now ask yourself this: are you seeing a mountain of dust or heaps of diamonds in the organization you are employed by? If your attitude is negative, the only thing you see is a pile of dust. This is why many employees complain about their organizations, but they still go to work every day.

Many people blame their parents, the system, and even their surroundings for their failure, when they are the ones responsible for it. I was born in a poor village to poor and illiterate parents with no basic amenities, so should I blame them? Of course not! In fact, the hardship that I experienced during my childhood became the main motivator for my success.

The village where I was born

10

We need to keep reminding ourselves that the only way to be successful is to have a positive attitude. Money doesn't like to come to people who have negative attitudes. Even if it does come, it disappears quickly. So remember this: a positive attitude is a person's passport to a better life.

The third factor is mind-set. Millions of people around the world dream of becoming millionaires. Unfortunately, very few achieve that status. Research shows that this is not because they lack intelligence or because of bad luck or because they come from a poor family or because of their religion, skin color, or gender, but because of their mind-set.

Let me tell you the difference between the poor and the rich. Poor people's minds are stuck here on the ground, thinking only about daily concerns and the here and now, while the minds of the rich are soaring in the clouds, like an eagle looking for opportunities to pounce on. So which group do you belong to?

**BAM factors: barriers that prevent many people
from being free to choose their own paths**

Remember that a negative mind-set is *a deadly poison right inside you*. It can do a lot of damage and literally can block your path to success. Success doesn't occur on its own. It doesn't come easy. It requires you to dream big and to have a specific plan, specific knowledge, the willingness to work hard, and the will to never give up. To do that, you need to have a clear and productive mind, because success begins with a state of mind. It is very important for you to understand your mind, because your thoughts create your reality. What you think is what you experience (see diagram below).

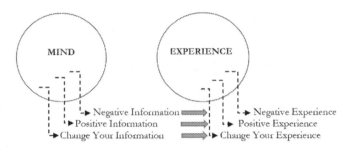

When you think negative thoughts, you have negative experiences. When you think positive thoughts, you have positive experiences. So to experience a positive change, you need to change negative thoughts and information into positive ones. I can't do this for you. Only you can do it!

The Story of a Farmer

Allow me to share the story of a farmer. When the farmer plants his crops, he does it at the best possible time in the correct season. Even then he doesn't just go into the field and sow his precious seed. Having the right time of the year and the land to plant it in is only a part of this important process. He spends much of his time using the plow, turning the ground, and removing the weeds that are the natural enemy of his crop. Then he does more tilling so the seeds can drive their tender young roots deep into the soft earth to have the best chance to flourish. There may not be enough fertilizer, or other additives may be needed to bring the soil to the correct balance. Only when the time is right, only when the soil is right, only when the weather is right will the farmer plant his crop.

In contrast, many of us want to change our negative mind-sets without preparing our inner ground. We plant seeds (positive and new ideas) in a hostile environment that has all sorts of opposing negative ideas that are already established. These dubious crops may be weeds that were planted during a painful experience, choking the new crop and limiting its success.

We just throw our seeds and then wonder why they fail. Did you know that we would all be starving if the farmers of the world did the same? We must all learn from the farmers, preparing our mental ground, breaking up our inner world, feeding it, opening our minds to new possibilities. Only then is success within our reach.

As farmers, we must get rid of the weeds (negative mind-sets and ideas) that grow in our inner fields, holding us back and restricting our creation of wealth. We must tend and feed our subconscious fields so we can transform our lives forever. Remember, never does a day go by without a number of changes taking place in our lives. We can choose to control the type of changes we make, or we can allow someone else to make choices for us. We can either choose to let things happen or choose to make things happen. So start making things happen in your life!

Turn Negative into Positive

Allow me to share with you my own experience of dealing with a negative mind-set. In 2007, a close friend cheated me out of $17,000. I had spent almost eight years saving the money, and it's all I had. I still haven't recovered it. It was a very frustrating and expensive experience, knowing that I had lost all my savings. I could have blamed myself for allowing someone to cheat me, but would blaming myself help my situation? Definitely not, and doing so would have made me more depressed. What did I do instead? I turned it into a lesson: do not trust anyone when it involves money.

Perhaps you too have experienced negative and unpleasant situations before. If you have, now is the time for you to turn the negative experiences into something positive. This is important, because thinking positively and having a positive mind-set creates motivation, which is the internal combustion within the mind that keeps the flywheel of belief turning and the body moving.

If you fuel your mind with positive directions, ambitions, and desires, there is nothing you can't achieve. So don't cry over your bad experiences and feel sorry for yourself. Feeling sorry for yourself is one of the major obstacles to making yourself shine and being successful. Turn the bad, ugly, and negative experiences into a positive force that pushes you forward to achieve your goals. In fact, the most important ingredients that drove me toward success were the hardships that I had experienced during my youth and the powerful urge to get my parents out of poverty.

Now ask yourself this: what are the most powerful drivers that can help to push you forward to achieve your goals? Write these in the box below to remind yourself.

```
Drivers:



```

Success Is about Taking Action

Now that you know the three factors that can hinder your progress, it is time to tackle them. To address these three factors successfully, you will need to execute your Personal Life Plan (PLP).

So what is a PLP? It is the blueprint you will need to catapult you to success. Don't just glance through it as if you are reading the Sunday news. Your PLP needs *action*. Remember, success is about taking *action*. When you take action, you engage all your six senses (sight, hearing, taste, smell, touch, and mind or intuition), and these are translated into power that produces results.

Remember the adage "If you fail to plan, you are planning to fail." Life is not about relying on luck or waiting for somebody else to give you an opportunity. But—and this is the sad truth—the majority of people never plan what they want to do with their lives. They just make the best of what they have and end up saying, "I'm just not lucky." Does that sound familiar to you?

Don't let luck determine your future. If you want to live your dream, you need a life plan. You need to be in control. You can't run your life on autopilot, but unfortunately that's exactly what the majority of the people do.

The purpose of your PLP is to make an impressive belief-, attitude-, and mind-changing impact on your life as you seriously consider the following:

- What do you really want?
- Why do you want it?
- How badly do you want it?
- When do you want it?

These thought-provoking questions will help to produce an exciting and credible overview of your life. They will also help you to know the purpose and objective of your future life and help you to establish the desired outcome for every area of your life through your personal life plan.

Your Personal Life Plan

To develop an effective personal life plan, it is important to understand the power of why, what, when, and how (see page 17). As you develop your personal life plan, you must ask yourself the following questions:

- Where am I right now in terms of career, savings, investment plans, and my overall financial standing?
- How will I get to where I want to be?
- What am I willing to sacrifice and do to get to where I want to be?
- When will I plan to get to where I want to be?

These why, what, when, and how questions will help you develop your Personal Life Plan.

This is the Life Plan of: _____ (your name)

Date: _____

The Why Questions
Why do you want a change in your
life?
Why do you want more than you
currently have?
Why do you think you're entitled to
more?
Why do you think you don't have
what you want now?

The What Questions
What do you want?
What do you have that you want to
get rid of?
What are you prepared to do to get
what you want?
What obstacles are you facing
now?

The When Questions
When do you need to achieve your
goals?
When do you need to get out of
your present circumstances?
When did you decide to do
something about your present
circumstances?
When did you last try to change
your present circumstances?

The How Questions
How can you achieve more
compared to previous years?
How can you overcome the failures
you experienced in the past?
How can you be sure of your future
success?
How much effort are you prepared
to put into achieving your goals?

The most challenging questions are "How would you know that your life plan works?" And "How would you know if you have achieved some success?" As with any plan, it takes time to see positive results, and these results can be achieved only by diligently working on your plan—*by taking action!*

Assume that you put your plan into action, and after a year it is time for you to do a progress review. Below are seven items that you must review to know your progress.

Item Descriptions	Yes	No
Are you experiencing less stress (financially) compared to the previous year?		
Do you have more disposable income now?		
Do you always pay all your bills on time?		
Do you put funds aside for your children's education?		
Do you have extra cash for investing?		
Are you acquiring residential or commercial properties or land?		
Do you regularly take your family for holiday trips?		

If you answered *yes* to all seven questions, congratulations to you; you are in good shape financially. However, if after reviewing your PLP and answering all seven questions, your progress shows less than 50 percent (that is, you answered yes to only two or three questions), you need to revisit your plan and look at the effort and action you put in. It could be that you have not been putting in 100 percent of the effort needed to make your plan work.

Take Life Seriously and Face Challenges

Don't take life for granted, because life is a serious matter. If you are not taking life seriously, your life is akin to a living death. Did you know that many people are already "dead" and only waiting to be buried? Look around, and you will see many miserable faces. Ask them what their hope is, and they will tell you that they have nothing to hope for. They are the living dead! And, unfortunately, they will inflict their children with their deadly and hopeless disease.

It is a common human reaction to avoid the unknown and the difficult. But if you want to achieve growth, fulfillment, and happiness, you must be willing to face challenges regularly. Never choose to remain stuck in a rut, craving certainty and security. In fact, security is an illusion. The only things certain in life are change, uncertainty, and death. Refusing to take on challenges does not guarantee security any more than hiding under the covers does. It simply stops you from learning, growing, and achieving your goals.

To be successful, you must be ready to experience a certain amount of discomfort, or even pain, as you tackle the challenges that offer you opportunities for fulfillment. Breaking free from self-imposed limitations, unsatisfactory circumstances, fears, habits, and beliefs is not easy. I have experienced it. I have felt it. I have endured, and I have conquered them all!

It is important to recognize the natural resistance you feel as you step out of your comfort zone and push your boundaries to further challenge yourself to see how far you can go. (Look at the Million-Dollar Challenge in appendix C to see which level you can achieve and how far you can go.)

But let me remind you that it is not necessary, or positive, to take on challenges just for the sake of it. Listen to your heart, and take action in a certain direction when you truly know that it's the way your higher self is leading you. If something feels wrong, it probably is. If something feels right but terrifying, dig deep within yourself for courage, and take the challenge. I am sure you will win.

Be Willing to Stretch Your Wings and Soar Higher

Avoiding challenges does not prevent discomfort. Being trapped and stifled can be more painful than the brief, intense pain that can come when you break free from your shackles and break out of your shell. It can even be soul destroying.

It was very difficult for me to learn and grow and be successful. The desire to give up constantly appeared. The feelings of self-doubt, fear, embarrassment, and uncertainty constantly filled every cell in my brain, making me feel that I could not achieve my dreams and goals. But the more obstacles and difficulties I faced, the more I was willing to stretch my wings in order to soar higher. I moved forward because I believed that if I kept doing only what came easily and naturally, I would never develop the skills needed to conquer the more difficult tasks.

Although I encourage you to stretch your wings, this doesn't mean you can leap out of the swamps of mediocrity and race straight to the mountaintop. As it is for most successful people, one step at a time is the way to reach even the highest peak. Don't be afraid of failing, because without failure you will not learn what doesn't work. If you fail, it doesn't mean it's the end of the world. If you fail, it just means that you shouldn't give up. FAIL means *First Attempt In Learning,* and you still have many chances to try until you succeed.

Don't Give Up Easily

If you were to achieve instant success in every challenge, it would be sheer luck. So remember that in whatever situation you are facing, there are always more things that don't work than things that do. Did you know that Thomas Edison failed over nine thousand times before perfecting the light bulb? How many of us would have given up at two failures, twenty failures, 150 failures, or at nine thousand failures? I believe many give up just after one failure. If you do, you will never achieve success.

If you want to succeed, your failures will give you valuable insight into methods that are more likely to succeed. Napoleon Hill, in his book *Think and Grow Rich*, says, "I will persist until I succeed." So if you want to be successful, don't give up easily, and don't take no for an answer. You must persist until you succeed!

Stay Focused

By a process of elimination, faith and persistence, hard work and determination, you can find the route to success. If I can do it, you can do it too.

Let's face it; most of us will not make millions of dollars a year, and the odds are that most of us won't receive a large windfall either. But that doesn't mean we can't build sizeable wealth. Building wealth takes time, and you must be determined and stay focused on your dreams and goals. If you are young, time is on your side, and retiring a millionaire is achievable. But if you are no longer young, don't be discouraged, because you can still make it when you are given the proven strategy and method.

One thing to remember is never to allow yourself to be swayed by anyone. You are on the way to success now, so stay focused. Remember this: an eagle never goes after two rabbits at the same time, but focuses on one rabbit and goes for the kill. So stay focused on a single goal at a time to hit your target.

I was helpless, hopeless, disoriented, frustrated, and buried in debts; I was even on the verge of committing suicide. But with a proven strategy and method and with a positive attitude, determination, hard work, and focus, I was able to create substantial wealth. Therefore, don't give up yet, as you might not have tried hard enough.

Before I conclude this chapter, I want to emphasize that to achieve significant levels of success, you need to possess the following traits:

- Passion: You should love what you do.
- Work: Take your work seriously and always work hard.
- Focus: Be like an eagle; focus on one thing and go for the kill.
- Push: Keep pushing yourself, even when you face numerous challenges and obstacles.
- Ideas: Come up with some good ideas, and capitalize on them.
- Improve: Keep improving yourself and what you do.
- Serve: Serve others something of value, and make them happy.
- Persist: Be persistent, because there is no overnight success. If there is, it is just an illusion.

In the next seven chapters are tried, tested, and proven strategies to wealth creation. These strategies will become the most powerful tools that you can have to help you build the wealth that you truly deserve. The last two chapters, "The Wealth Blueprint" and "The Power of Investing," show how the wealth you have created can last for a very long time.

I must remind you that these strategies are not the cure to your financial problems, especially if you fail to understand the wisdom behind them. The strategies are effective only for those who understand their wisdom and put them into practice.

It is always important to remind ourselves that success doesn't come easy, but when we know what we are aiming for, taking the shot is much easier. Now let the wisdom of wealth creation strategies be bestowed upon you on this wonderful journey that I call the wealth en*rich*ment journey.

Key Takeaways

Think about the things you will take away from chapter 2 and how and when you will implement them. For example, remember the BAM triangle—belief, attitude, and mind-set—and indicate when you will start working on making those three factors work to your advantage.

Topic	Takeaways	Implementation
The BAM Triangle	Belief, attitude, and mind-set	
Turn Negative into Positive		
Your Success Drivers		
What is PLP?		
Be Willing to Stretch Your Wings and Soar Higher		

Chapter 3

Strategy 1
Pay Yourself First

The secret of getting ahead is getting started.

Mark Twain

It's almost the end of the month. Do you know who you are paying? Of course you do, because you have a long list of bills to pay to avoid getting into trouble. For example, you have to pay for your utilities, insurance, groceries, telephone, satellite TV—and the list goes on and on.

Now, did you miss anyone? I bet you missed paying yourself. But how can you miss *that*?

This first strategy—paying yourself—is important, because no one can build substantial wealth without firmly establishing himself or herself in this first strategy. It is the foundation for the next six strategies (see illustration below).

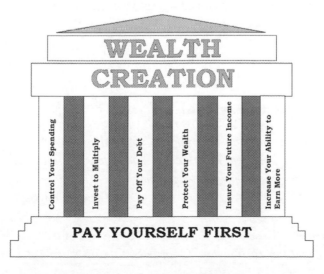

As an Employee, You Can Be Wealthy Too

Have you ever imagined that you can create wealth as an employee or as a salary earner? When I asked myself that question fourteen years ago, I was very skeptical. I had convinced myself that there was no way I could create wealth as a salary earner. Yet I was telling the audiences in my motivational seminars they could. I was behaving like most politicians; I wasn't walking the talk.

Then one day I decided to start my own business. I thought this would bring the financial freedom I had been looking for. While running my business, I didn't quit my regular job, as I still needed the stable income my job brought. After a few years in business, I started to feel the heat. The business world is indeed very tough, especially when you don't have the financial backup. Without capital, it was hard to take my business to the next level. The worst part was when debtors paid late, but my bills and employees' salaries couldn't wait. It was game over for me.

The moment I quit my business, I decided to walk my talk. The first thing I did was work on my Personal Life Plan (see chapter 2). I answered all the questions in the PLP as honestly as I could. After that, I diligently executed the seven key strategies. After a year, I checked my progress against the Wealth Blueprint (see chapter 10). Once I saw the positive results, I was convinced it was possible to create wealth, even though I was just an employee. So don't underestimate your status as an employee.

Let's get started. Here is the first strategy.

Don't Forget to Pay Yourself

> *It's not how much money you make, but how much money you keep, how hard it works for you, and how many generations you keep it for.*
>
> Robert Kiyosaki

This is the wealth strategy that has stood the test of time. In his book *The Richest Man in Babylon*, George S. Clason said, "Gold cometh gladly and in increasing quantity to any man who will put not less than one-tenth of his earnings to create an estate for his future and that of his family." What he meant was that you need to pay yourself no less than 10 percent of your salary and invest it before you pay anything else.

In many of my motivational seminars, I tell the audience that before they pay all their debts, they must pay themselves. By paying themselves at least 10 percent of their salary, they start to build the foundation of their wealth.

Paying yourself is the foundation of wealth creation.

What happens if you don't pay yourself? Not only will you fail to build the foundation for your wealth, but you won't get motivated and do your best. If you worked for me, at the end of the month you'd expect to get paid. If I couldn't pay you, how would you feel? You would be disappointed, right? Maybe you would continue to work for me a second month. But toward the end of your second month, I told you again that I wouldn't pay you for a reason only known to me. How would you feel? Frustrated? Disappointed? Like you want to harm me? I can understand your frustration. Will you come back to work for me for a third month? I bet you would not. And you might report me to the authorities for ripping you off. But sadly, many people keep working month after month despite not being paid. Guess what. The first "person" you pay is the utility company, water company, your bank, and the list goes on and on. You keep doing this every month, and you still fail to pay yourself. How can you become rich and create wealth for yourself and your family if you fail to pay yourself? And how long are you going to do it? This is the time for you to correct this mistake. It is time to pay yourself! Start right now, because if you don't, you will end up like Steven instead of like John in the stories below.

How a Modest Salary Made John Wealthy

This is a story of John, who is a millionaire despite never earning a large income. John began working at age twenty-two, soon after graduating from college. Although his starting salary was fairly low after graduation, he managed to live well below his means. John committed to investing at least 10 percent of his income and avoided using credit cards. Through hard work and dedication, he has worked his way to a management position and now earns $70,000 a year.

John's family lives a simple life, and they have stayed in their small, three-bedroom house in a working-class neighborhood. John and his wife paid off their mortgage a few years ago. Their children attended public schools, and when the kids grew up and needed cars, they bought used cars and paid cash.

John's family may not live a lavish lifestyle, but they are not only comfortable, they are debt-free. And after twenty-eight years of investing 10 percent of his income, John has built up an investment portfolio worth close to $1.5 million. With a simple annual budget of $50,000, his family could sustain their current lifestyle for more than thirty years, without John or his wife ever having to work again.

How Steven Went Broke

Despite earning three times more than John, Steven is suffering financially; he is broke. This is how the story goes. Steven is a partner in a large law firm, and he earns a large income—three times that of John. Unlike John, he attended an expensive private university, and after his graduation he was already in debt to the tune of over $200,000 in student loans.

Steven is a very intelligent and hardworking lawyer, and with his excellent track record, he was made a junior partner earning over $200,000 annually. With the comfort of a high salary, Steven's family lives extremely well. He qualified for a huge mortgage on a $1,000,000 home in an exclusive gated community. Steven's children attend prestigious local private schools, and he and his wife drive the latest imported luxury vehicles.

As Steven became more successful and commanded high respect among his business partners and the legal fraternity, he was given a substantial raise; his annual salary increased to $370,000. Unfortunately, Steven was suffering financially because his expenses were also high due to the large mortgage payments, payments on three credit cards, payments on two luxury cars, his children's private school fees, his own student loans, club memberships, luxury clothing, expensive vacations, and expensive entertainment.

Most months, Steven and his family's spending and expenses exceed his income. Because of his failing financial health, Steven's work performance is affected. In fact, his family is living from paycheck to paycheck, despite his huge annual salary.

Because of his huge commitments, Steven was not able to pay himself 10 percent of his salary. If he were to stop working, his family would soon be destitute.

Lesson Learned

What is the lesson we can learn from the stories above? John's story tells us that even as employees earning a modest salary, we can create substantial wealth if we live within our means and pay ourselves 10 percent of our income by investing that money.

On the other hand, Steven's story reminds us that even if you are highly paid, if you spend more than you earn, you will end up in debt and live your life broke.

Look at two different scenarios. You can either enjoy now and suffer later or save and invest now and enjoy later. The choice is yours.

Your Commitment Is Your Wealth

One thing for sure is that your real wealth is a result of your commitment not the money. Remember, when you receive your salary at the end of the month, the very first thing you need to do is immediately take out 10 percent from your gross income to pay yourself. *This is your commitment!* Why gross income? Because gross income will contribute more toward your wealth, compared to net income, where income taxes and other deductions have already been made.

Be the First Recipient of Your Salary

Before you pay all your creditors, you must pay yourself 10 percent first. You should be the first recipient of that salary. Assume that your gross salary is $5,000 per month. The first thing you do is to take out 10 percent—so you pay yourself $500 per month without exception. This $500 must be saved; don't touch this money. Put it in an investment account that earns you interest of at least 7 to 8 percent annually. Don't put this money in your savings account, where you have easy access via your ATM card. Moreover, putting this money in your saving account will not bring the interest that you want.

You must pay yourself every month. Over twelve months you will be able to accumulate $6,000 (12 × $500). This amount will be more with interest earned on interest. (This is called compound interest.) If you don't do this, you will never save a single cent for the whole twelve months.

Now you can see how much money you have saved by just paying yourself 10 percent per month. At the end of twelve months, you are $6,000 richer and more with 8 percent interest. (If you can't even pay yourself 10 percent every month, see appendix A for a simple way to save $13,780 per year—getting you started in creating your wealth.)

For the last five years I have committed my life to this strategy—paying myself even more than 10 percent every month. I have stuck to it every month without fail, and my cash flow has improved tremendously. Best of all is a sense of relief knowing that I have financial backup if one day I need it. By paying myself, I realized that life has more meaning. I started to enjoy my work, knowing that I will be paid at the end of the month.

You Must Stay on Course

Remember, to be successful in creating your wealth, you need to stay on course. Successful investors will tell you the same thing: success comes from patience, diligence, and perseverance more than anything else. Brilliance and aggressiveness are more likely to cost you than to add anything to your wealth account. Even billionaire Warren Buffett said that the secret of his success was that he mastered "the art of doing nothing"—his phrase for doing simple things and being patient.

The Power of Compounding

Let compounding do its work by giving it time and staying out of its way. Remember, even if you start with small investments to begin with, such as $500 a month ($6,000 annually), after thirty years and with the power of compound interest (8 percent), your investment will grow to a sizable sum ($750,147.59)—if you stay the course (see table on page 32).

Year	Deposits	Interest	Balance
1	$6,000.00	$266.46	$6,266.46
2	$6,000.00	$786.58	$13,053.04
3	$6,000.00	$1,349.86	$20,402.90
4	$6,000.00	$1,959.89	$28,362.79
5	$6,000.00	$2,620.56	$36,983.35
6	$6,000.00	$3,336.06	$46,319.41
7	$6,000.00	$4,110.95	$56,430.36
8	$6,000.00	$4,950.16	$67,380.52
9	$6,000.00	$5,859.01	$79,239.53
10	$6,000.00	$6,843.30	$92,082.84
11	$6,000.00	$7,909.29	$105,992.13
12	$6,000.00	$9,063.76	$121,055.89
13	$6,000.00	$10,314.04	$137,369.93
14	$6,000.00	$11,668.10	$155,038.03
15	$6,000.00	$13,134.54	$174,172.57
16	$6,000.00	$14,722.70	$194,895.27
17	$6,000.00	$16,442.67	$217,337.95
18	$6,000.00	$18,305.41	$241,643.35
19	$6,000.00	$20,322.74	$267,966.09
20	$6,000.00	$22,507.52	$296,473.61
21	$6,000.00	$24,873.63	$327,347.24
22	$6,000.00	$27,436.12	$360,783.36
23	$6,000.00	$30,211.30	$396,994.66
24	$6,000.00	$33,216.82	$436,211.48
25	$6,000.00	$36,471.80	$478,683.29
26	$6,000.00	$39,996.94	$524,680.22
27	$6,000.00	$43,814.66	$574,494.89
28	$6,000.00	$47,949.26	$628,444.14
29	$6,000.00	$52,427.02	$686,871.16
30	$6,000.00	$57,276.43	$750,147.59
Totals	$180,000.00	$570,147.59	$750,147.59

The future value of 360 monthly deposits of $500, deposited at the beginning of each period and earning an annual interest rate of 8 percent would be $750,147.59—of which $180,000 is the total of the deposits and $570,147.59 is the total interest earned. The $570,147.59

also represents the financial opportunity cost of spending $500 per month for thirty years on nonessential expenditures that lose their value with time and/or use.

You see, making investing through saving is not rocket science; it amounts to paying yourself first every month, even if you have to do without some small things in the short term.

Give Yourself a Pay Raise

The reason you give yourself a pay raise is to increase the amount you save so that you can accumulate wealth fast. It is quite simple: you do it through self-appraisal. You need to appraise yourself based on four performance ratings: E for Exceptional, EE for exceeding expectations, M for meeting expectations, and U for unsatisfactory (see table on page 34). In this case the reward is different from the reward for your performance given to you by your company. Your company—the employer—will compensate you with a higher increment if you get E and no increment if you only get U. But in this case, if you get U, you will need to contribute more.

Here is how it works. Assume you have not deducted 10 percent from your salary for the past twelve months; you will then be appraised as U (unsatisfactory). The "punishment" is having to start to increase your deduction by an additional 7 percent, making your total deduction from your salary 17 percent per month (10 percent plus 7 percent). This will punish you in that you will have less disposal income so that you can catch up with your wealth creation plan.

If you have deducted 10 percent from your salary every month for the last twelve months, you can reward your excellent performance by deducting only an additional 2 percent, making your total deduction 12 percent every month from the second year onward. In this case, you have more disposable income to enjoy with your family. This is your reward for successfully executing your wealth creation plan.

However, EE indicated that you missed deducting no more than three months, so in second year, your total deduction will be 13 percent (10 percent plus 3 percent). The M indicated that you have missed the deduction of four months to eleven months. Therefore, in the second year your total deduction will be 15 percent (10 percent plus 5 percent). In the third year, start the self-appraisal again. By doing this, you will ensure your deduction increases as your income increases. The positive outcome of this is a tremendous increase in your accumulated capital investment. You are on track to achieving your financial goals.

Self-Appraisal

Appraisal	E	EE	M	U
Percentage	2	3	5	7

Remember to Pay Yourself Every Month

Keep this in mind: for you to be able to see your wealth grow, it is of utmost importance that you pay yourself every month. Don't ever negotiate yourself out of it. Remind yourself that wealth creation is your main goal and that you must stick to it for a long time. Don't get distracted easily, because to achieve any success in life demands your long-term commitment and focus.

Remember Colonel Sanders (the founder of Kentucky Fried Chicken)? When he was sixty-five, he was broke and living in his car. The only thing he had of any value was a recipe. He had to knock on 1,009 doors before someone agreed to his deal—to give him a royalty from every piece of chicken cooked with his recipe. His wife kept the statistics.

I am not Colonel Sanders, but I can give you the recipe. And the good thing is I am not asking you to pay me a royalty from every penny you save based on my recipe. When you are already rich and see me around town, just buy me a cup of coffee. I will be extremely happy for your success.

Summary

I want to remind you again that the *secret to wealth creation is not how much you earn but how much you save.* It is a commitment and a sacrifice. You must save at least 10 percent every month, and this is your commitment. If you think you can't, you have to sacrifice something to get that 10 percent. Remember, the more sacrifices you make now and the more committed you are, the more you will save and the more you will make at the end of the day. But with no sacrifice and no commitment, you will have no money and no life; you will be just a living corpse waiting to be disposed of, and no one wants to be associated with a living corpse. Definitely not me!

Key Takeaways

Think about the things you will take away from strategy 1 and how and when you will implement them. For example, under the topic "Pay Yourself," the takeaway is "Start deducting 10 percent from your salary." For implementation, you need to indicate the date when you will start paying yourself 10 percent.

Topic	Takeaways	Implementation
Pay Yourself	Start deducting 10 percent from your salary.	
Your Wealth Commitment		
The Power of Compounding		
Pay Raise		

Chapter 4

Strategy 2
Control Your Spending

*The urge to spend all you make is called consumer
mentality. Try to get investment mentality instead.*
                                        Edward H. Romney

Most people believe the key to wealth is a high-paying job. Yes, it's easier to amass assets if you have more money coming in each month, but the true secret to increasing your net worth is to **spend less than you make**. But if you live way beyond your means and are spending your hard-earned cash on goods and services that you want but don't necessarily need, you are inviting trouble. You need to realize that even relatively small expenses can really add up.

In this chapter, I will describe the golden rule of wealth creation and why it is important not to break it. I will also show the differences between needs and wants, and I will present some techniques you can use to track your expenses and spending.

The Golden Rule

The golden rule of wealth creation is to *spend less than you earn*. (Underline this statement!) It is a very simple rule, but so many people ignore it, especially the poor and middle class.

Golden Rule: Spend less than you earn.

As a rule of thumb, your spending or expenses should be below the remaining 90 percent of your salary. Ideally, it should be about 80 percent so you have the balance of 10 percent in which you invest in a high-risk portfolio. (See the salary [S] and expense [E] thermometer below.)

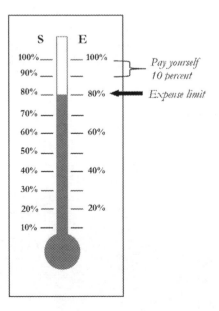

Financial Statements of the Poor and the Rich

This is what poor people's financial statement and rich people's financial statement look like. Can you see the difference?

Poor People's
Financial Statement

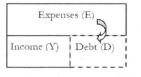

Rich People's
Financial Statement

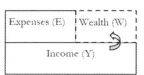

In the poor people's financial statement, you can see expenses exceeding income, which results in debt. While in the rich people's financial statement, you see income exceeding expenses, which results in wealth.

Now it is time to check your financial statement to see which group you belong to. Are you in the poor people's category or the rich people's category? I can't emphasize this enough: if you want to create wealth, you need to watch your spending and expenses and make sure they are not exceeding your income. If they are, you need to cut unnecessary expenses, because most likely they are incurred to fulfill your wants rather than needs. I have been down this path before, and as a result I was buried in a mountain of debt.

Poor and the Rich People's Accounts

Let's see the differences between poor people's accounts and rich people's accounts (see diagram on page 40). As you can see from the poor people's account, most of the income (Y) flows into the expense account (E), which then creates debt (D) or liabilities, and nothing is left for investment (I). In the rich people's account, most of the income (Y) flows into an investment account (I), which creates wealth (W).

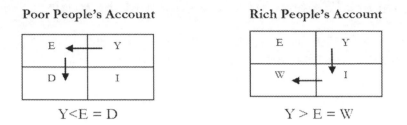

Poor People's Account   Rich People's Account

$$Y<E = D \qquad\qquad Y > E = W$$

If your account is like the poor people's account right now, start looking at your expenses and spending, and do something about it. If it was an extra car that caused your expense account to inflate, consider selling the car. If your entertainment expenses or your impulse spending habits put you into debt, stop the habit. The bottom line is that you need to realize that even relatively small expenses can really add up.

Don't Break the Golden Rule of Wealth Creation

If your goal is to create wealth, don't break this golden rule. One way to avoid breaking it is to limit your spending on your wants. For instance, the simple strategy for me to avoid breaking the golden rule is to always carry a card in my wallet with the words "Golden Rule: Spend Less than I Earn." This card is next to my credit card. So when I decide to use my credit card, my golden rule card comes out first as a reminder.

Limiting your spending on your wants will definitely allow you to create a little bit of savings with which to generate more income. My advice is that you always reassess your needs and try to avoid fulfilling your wants. Ask yourself or your spouse questions with all honesty. For instance, do you or your spouse really need the new mobile phone or new handbag or new shoes or even a new pair of trousers or a blouse? I know we have two ears, but one phone is sufficient. And I don't think you need many pairs of shoes unless you have extra feet.

Count the shirts or dresses or blouses you never wear. How many handbags are still wrapped in the plastic bag? How many pairs of shoes do you wear only once a year or never wear at all. Buying all these extra things that you don't need puts a big hole in your pocket. It is better for you to invest the money and let it grow to earn you more money. This is a smart investment strategy as opposed to showing off for nothing. Always remember this: *It is not about how much you earn. It is how much you save that counts.* Highlight this statement, as this is an important reminder.

This is not based on information I got from magazines or books, but on my own life experience. Allow me to tell you about myself and my collection of antique cars. Many years back, I loved to spend my extra cash buying antique cars. I wasted money not only to acquire those cars, but also to make the cars look nice. After a while, I lost interest in them and wanted to get rid of them, even at a loss, because they were too expensive to maintain.

Do I need many cars? No, I don't. Have I wasted money buying these cars, which I seldom drive? Yes, I have. Is this a good investment? Absolutely not, and I lost money as well as interest. Did I learn a lesson from this expensive mistake? Absolutely, and that is why I can share my experience with you so that you will not make the same mistake that I made—that is, fulfilling wants rather than needs.

Needs and Wants

> *Before you make any purchase, ask yourself if you really need it. In most cases your life won't be any less full or rich without it.*
>
> Kim McKay and Jenny Bonin

What are the differences between needs and wants? A need is something you must have and can't do without. In actuality, you need only four things to survive:

- a roof over your head
- enough food and water to maintain your health
- basic health care and hygiene products
- clothing for you to stay comfortable and appropriately dressed

Everything that goes beyond these four things, such as a big house, brand-name clothes, fancy foods and drinks, and a new car, are your wants. A want is something you would like to have, but you can survive without it. In fact, if you try to fulfill unlimited wants with limited money, you will end up with liabilities.

If you want to become wealthy, start adopting a disciplined lifestyle and budget. This doesn't mean that you can't go out and have fun, but you should try to do things in moderation and set a budget if you hope to save money. Stop trying to impress people around you. And stop trying to compete with your friends and neighbors; doing so will expand your liabilities account.

I observe unhealthy competition like this frequently when people buy new furniture and curtains on impulse to impress their friends, neighbors, and visitors. But ask yourself, *Is this furniture and are these curtains my wants* (to impress) *or my needs* (because you have to replace the old furniture and curtains)? There is really no point in living a life full of stress because of financial problems that you can easily avoid. Always remember to live by the principle of making your wants less than your needs.

Track Your Cash Flow

One way to know whether you are spending on wants rather than needs is by tracking your cash flow. When I was deeply in debt, I was avoiding tracking my cash flow at all costs. I was afraid to face the reality when it came to liabilities. But that was one of the most costly mistakes I made. For the same reason, my advice to you is to track your cash flow. It is much better to face the reality rather than avoid it, as it will bite you later.

What is cash flow? Cash flow is money coming in (what you earn) and money going out (what you spend). If you run out of money before the next payday, you know you have a cash flow problem.

Many people assume that the problem is that they don't make enough money, when the reality is that they can't control their spending to match their income. I can't stress this more: **you need to**

keep track of your income and spending. You need to know how much you earn and where the other sources of income are coming from and what your expenses are. You also need to know about any expenditure that is likely to come and any provision you have made for contingencies. These are all very important pieces of information for your financial planning. Not knowing this is the biggest mistake, because it translates to ignorance and not knowing what you are doing, where you are financially, and what is ahead of you. This is very dangerous for your future.

I can't emphasize this more: it is worth keeping track of your income, spending, and expenses because constantly living in debt is not fun at all. I have experienced it, and I don't want to experience it again. If you are constantly living in debt, you know what I mean. Remember the story I shared in the introductory chapter of this book about not having money to buy even a simple present for my children one Christmas. I let my children down because of my ignorance.

So don't be ignorant! It can be tough to control spending and keep track of all your expenses, but try to living in debt and feeling the stress all the time. Which do you prefer?

Cash Flow Worksheet

On the following page is a cash flow worksheet to help you track your expenses. Use this worksheet to monitor your spending for the next six months, and see your financial health improve.

Why six months? In six months you will have more information regarding your financial health. And with this information you will cultivate better habits; you will be able to differentiate between needs and wants. I am confident that even before six months have ended, you will become more aware of your spending habits. Try it, and see for yourself! I use this, and my wife doesn't like it, as I am now more mindful when it comes to spending.

Cash Flow Worksheet

No	Items	Month 1	Month 2	Month 3	Month 4	Month 5	Month 6
	Income						
	Salary						
	Other source						
A	**Total Income**						
	Expenses						
1	**Home**						
	Mortgage payment						
	Rent payment						
	Incidentals (supplies)						
	Furnishings						
	Other:						
	Sub-total						
2	**Food**						
	Groceries						
	Dining out						
	Parties						
	Other:						
	Sub-total						
3	**Clothing**						
	Clothing						
	Laundry						
	Other:						
	Sub-total						
4	**Vehicle**						
	Vehicle payment						
	Operating expenses (gas, oil, services, etc.)						
	Other maintenance						
	Other:						
	Sub-total						
5	**Personal Care**						
	Saloon expenses						
	Hair maintenance						
	Other:						
	Sub-total						

6	**Utilities**						
	Telephone (land line)						
	Mobile phone						
	Water						
	Electricity						
	Internet						
	Satellite TV						
	Other:						
	Sub-total						
7	**Entertainment**						
	Night out (clubbing)						
	Books, newspapers, etc.						
	Parties						
	Movies						
	Other:						
	Sub-total						
8	**Property Tax**						
	House						
	Land						
	Commercial properties						
	Other:						
	Sub-total						
9	**Unreimbursed Business Expenses**						
	Travel						
	Phones						
	Lodging						
	Parking						
	Meals						
	Other:						
	Sub-total						
10	**Children's Expenses**						
	Daycare						
	Tuition						
	Domestic help						
	Other:						
	Sub-total						

11	**Medical Expenses**						
	Medical expenses						
	Dental						
	Vision						
	Other:						
	Sub-total						
12	**Insurance**						
	Health						
	Vehicle						
	House						
	Life						
	Other:						
	Sub-total						
13	**Gifts**						
	Festive session						
	Birthday						
	Anniversaries						
	Other:						
	Sub-total						
14	**Charitable Contributions**						
	Charitable organization						
	Schools						
	Society						
	Other:						
	Sub-total						
15	**Liabilities**						
	Credit card						
	Personal loans						
	Business loans						
	Student loans						
	Other:						
	Sub-total						
B	**Total Expenses**						
C	**Net Cash Flow (A-B)**						

How are you doing with your net cash flow? Is it positive or negative? If your net cash flow is negative, what are you going to do? You must revisit your cash flow worksheet to see which expenses are wants and then eliminate or reduce them.

By keeping track of your cash flow, you will manage your income and spending better, and your financial health will improve. Trust me! The reason many people are constantly having liabilities is because they don't track their cash flow. It is not that they don't want to do it; the reality is they don't want to face the fact that some spending and expenses are unnecessary—just to fulfill their wants.

Many of my friends constantly complain about not having enough money and having lots of debts, but they still go out almost every night to have fun. Imagine how much money they waste on unnecessary entertainment expenses. I have seen some of them spend a few hundred—or even up to a thousand—for just one night.

I am not saying that you can't enjoy life, but wasting money every night and jeopardizing your financial health is not worth it. So always make it a habit to track your cash flow, because by doing so, you will know which expenses belong to the wants category. By eliminating your wants, you are not only avoiding putting yourself in debt, but you are also saving some money and investing it to create wealth. Remember, creating your wealth should be your goal.

Your Wheel of Fortune

A wheel of fortune is another way to see the shape of your financial health. This wheel has twelve spokes and four circles (see diagram on page 48). The middle or the smallest circle is called the hub of the wheel, and it is represented by A (never). The second circle is represented by B (rarely), the third circle is represented by C (sometimes), and finally the fourth circle is represented by D (always).

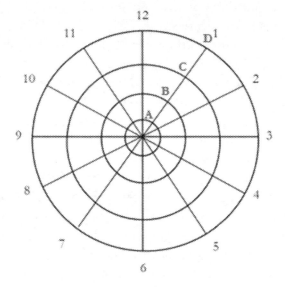

As you can see in the table below, there are twelve fortune descriptions, and these descriptions represent the twelve spokes mentioned earlier.

SN	Fortune Descriptions	Never A	Rarely B	Sometimes C	Always D
1	Do you pay yourself 10 percent of your salary every month?				
2	Do you stick to your shopping list when you go shopping?				
3	Do you always avoid using credit cards for your purchases?				
4	Do you pay your credit card in full every month?				
5	Do you regularly put aside 5 to 10 percent of your money for high risk investments?				
6	Do you have other sources of income besides your salary?				
7	Are you paying all your bills on time?				
8	Are you receiving passive income?				
9	Are you experiencing less stress compared to the previous year?				
10	How often do you take your family on holidays abroad?				
11	Are you acquiring residential or commercial properties or land?				
12	Are you putting funds aside for your children's education?				

Completing Your Wheel

Let's complete your wheel of fortune. The first step is to complete the table by answering all the questions (see table on page 48). For instance, for question 1, if you don't pay yourself 10 percent every month, you check the column "Never." Since "Never" equals A, mark an X on the smallest circle—that is, the first spoke. Once you have completed the table, place an X on each spoke according to any of the four answers that you selected. Do this now.

The Shape of Your Wheel

The next step is to join the Xs to make the shape of your wheel (complete figure 1). Once the shape is formed, think of it as the wheels of your car, and ask yourself if the car will run smoothly with such a wheel.

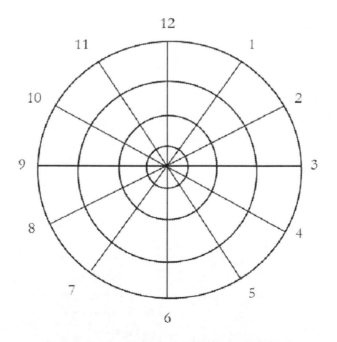

Figure 1: Completion of Fortune Wheel

Interpreting Your Wheel

Here is how to interpret you wheel of fortune. Take note that the shape of your wheel might be different from these shapes, but it gives an indication of which wheel you belong to.

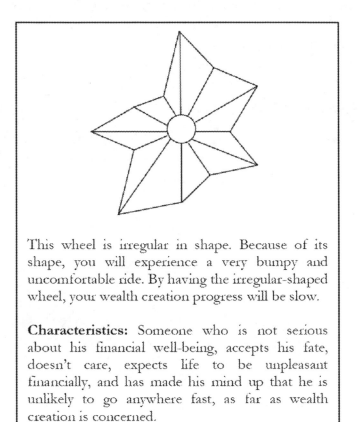

This wheel is irregular in shape. Because of its shape, you will experience a very bumpy and uncomfortable ride. By having the irregular-shaped wheel, your wealth creation progress will be slow.

Characteristics: Someone who is not serious about his financial well-being, accepts his fate, doesn't care, expects life to be unpleasant financially, and has made his mind up that he is unlikely to go anywhere fast, as far as wealth creation is concerned.

This wheel is also irregular in shape and has three sharp edges. Because of its shape and the pointed edges, the wheel is not only bumpy but very dangerous when it turns.

Characteristics: Someone who doesn't care about his financial future and is constantly living in debt. Despite his serious financial health problems, he has no real ambition to find a cure for them and has no plan to create wealth for his future descendants.

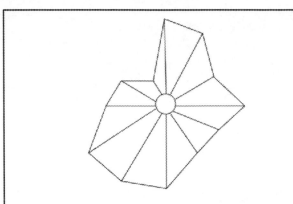

This is a large, uneven wheel. This wheel is bumpy when turning; it may cause a great deal of damage and is dangerous to those who use it.

Characteristics: Someone who tries to create his wealth but fails to plan accordingly. This person is generally disciplined regarding spending but very poor in managing his investments. He or she doesn't have constant sources of non-salary income. As a result, this person is trading his time for money and is not creating wealth from passive income streams.

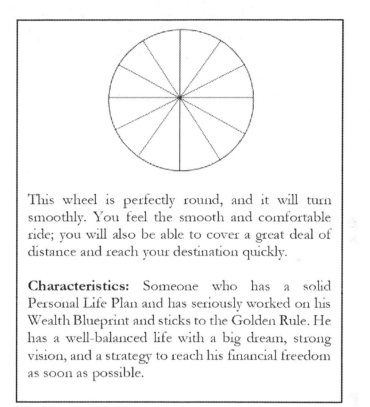

This wheel is perfectly round, and it will turn smoothly. You feel the smooth and comfortable ride; you will also be able to cover a great deal of distance and reach your destination quickly.

Characteristics: Someone who has a solid Personal Life Plan and has seriously worked on his Wealth Blueprint and sticks to the Golden Rule. He has a well-balanced life with a big dream, strong vision, and a strategy to reach his financial freedom as soon as possible.

So, what shape is your wheel? Take action now if your wheel is not perfectly round. If your wheel is perfectly round, keep moving and stay focused so that you can reach your financial goals as soon as possible. I know you can achieve your financial goals, and you must believe that too. Remember, the size of your success is determined by the size of your belief. Always aim high and shoot for the stars. Even if you fail to land on the moon, you still have the opportunity to land in the treetops.

Summary

To be able to accumulate wealth, always stick to the golden rule of wealth creation: spend less than you earn. To be able to do that, spend only on your needs, and limit your wants. Remember that the poor and middle class buy luxuries first, and they suffer financially, while the rich buy luxuries last, but they still enjoy their wealth.

It is also very important to keep track of your expenses so that you know your financial health and are able to take corrective action immediately, before it becomes cancerous. So, stop senseless spending, as it is not worth it.

Key Takeaways

Think about the things you will take away from strategy 2 and how and when you will implement them.

Topic	Takeaways	Implementation
Golden Rule		
Needs		
Wants		
Track Your Cash Flow		
The Wheel of Fortune		

Chapter 5

Strategy 3
Invest to Multiply

In any investment, you expect to have fun and make money.
Michael Jordan

Did you know that the wealth of the richest 1 percent of people in the world amounts to $110 trillion? That's sixty-five times the total wealth of the bottom half of the world's population. Where is this wealth coming from? It is coming from rich people's investments, and this is what this chapter is all about. This chapter presents the third strategy—that is, investing to multiply wealth.

It is important to remind yourself that your wealth is not measured by the amount of money you have in your pocket. Having money in your pocket can result in two possibilities. First, you might spend it all and go broke. Second, it will not multiply to give you more money, because you are not investing it. Your wealth can be created only by investing what you have in order to earn more money—making money work for you. This is what you should desire: an income that continues to flow in, whether you work or not.

Invest continuously to create more wealth.

The Tragedy of the Earn-and-Spend Cycle

Have you ever wondered how the rich get richer while the poor get poorer? Look around you at people over sixty or seventy years of age. How are they living? Chances are, you will see or know some who are barely scraping by and others who are living well. What is the difference between them? More likely than not, the difference between those who are rich and those who are poor is that rich people keep investing to multiply their wealth, while the poor do not; they spend every dollar they have.

The majority of poor people are trapped in the earn-and-spend cycle. If you are one of them, you need to break away from it. Did you know that many highly paid athletes earned hundreds of millions of dollars yet went bankrupt? Why did this happen? The main reason is because they were in the earn-and-spend cycle (see below).

The problem with the earn-and-spend cycle is that when you stop earning, you face financial difficulties because your spending and other financial obligations are still ongoing but your income stops. This happens to the majority of the employees who depend only on their salary to survive—that is, to cover all their expenses. When their income source is terminated, the lifestyle is also terminated, and this is a very scary scenario. But how many employees are well prepared for this? Are you well prepared?

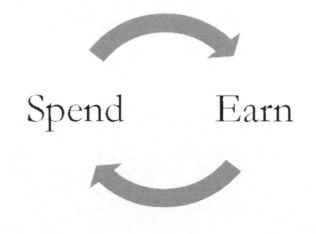

The Benefit of the Earn-and-Invest Cycle

To prevent a financial disaster, instead of getting trapped in the earn-and-spend cycle, you should be in the earn-and-invest cycle (see below). In the earn-and-invest cycle, spending is not ignored, but the emphasis is on investment—that is, paying yourself 10 percent or more every month and investing that money.

When there is an investment, we can expect a return on investment (ROI) that will further contribute to our earnings. In this case, even if your income stops, you will still earn from your investment. The income from your investment can help to sustain your spending and lifestyle. This is the benefit of the earn-and-invest cycle. So don't ignore this cycle. You *must* devote a good percentage (at least 10 percent) of your income to investment.

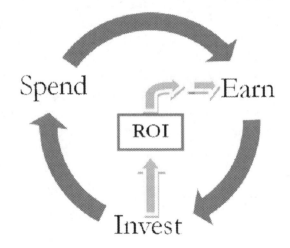

Did You Commit to Strategies 1 and 2?

Now ask yourself these questions:

- How much have you invested in the past two years?
- How much have you multiplied your wealth in the past two years?

Chances are you might not have done either in the past two years. That could be due to your lack of commitment to strategies 1 and 2, as discussed in chapters 3 and 4. Or perhaps you have committed to both strategies, but you are not sure how to deal with strategy 3. But don't worry, because this chapter will provide you with the know-how so you can invest successfully to multiply your wealth.

Your Investment Creed

What is your investment creed? Do you have one? You don't have to think too deeply about this. If you do, chances are you will not invest. In my experience, to be successful in investing, you need to think and make decisions fast, because if you don't, you might miss the opportunity.

When you are ready to invest, your mental arsenal should be similar to that of a samurai. The samurai lived by a simple creed: no fear, no doubt, no hesitation, and no surprise. Because their creed was simple to understand, it became their most brilliant strategy. When investing, be guided by your simple creed. And once you know everything you need to know and decide on a course of action, commit to it and get on with it as quickly as possible with no fear, no doubt, no hesitation—and avoiding surprise. Always remember to balance your risk appetite, and then go for it.

Take Action Fast

Remember, do not keep your money in your pocket or under a pillow. You should invest it to earn more money. And don't wait too long for the right opportunity, because you might miss it. In fact, acting fast can be a lot better than holding out on a possibility.

Let me share my recent investment deal. When I was introduced to a sale of residential land (two lots) in November 2014, without hesitation I immediately sealed the deal. After I paid the deposit, I was told that the price of similar lots next to mine would increase in January 2015 by few more thousands by the time goods and services tax (GST) was to be introduced in April 2015. So timing was very important. Like the samurai, I needed to act swiftly, and the most important thing was to commit to a course of action.

Investment Strategies

Investing should be more like watching paint dry or watching grass grow. If you want excitement, take $800 and go to Las Vegas.

Paul Samuelson

To continue building your wealth, you must continue to invest. As I said earlier, you want your money to earn more money for you. In this way you can create your wealth fast. I know that investing be intimidating for people who have little or no experience and knowledge in it. But don't allow that lack to stop you from investing your money. Here are three simple strategies to ensure successful investment.

- **Listen actively.** Always seek and listen to the advice of your financial adviser. Don't try to become an expert yourself, because investing is not gambling. Investing requires planning and patience. Therefore, choose your financial adviser based on his or her credentials and professionalism (experience, knowledge, duration in the market or how long he or she has been with a particular company, and after-sales service). I would not choose a financial adviser who is just a good friend. Don't mix business with friendship.

    If you don't trust a particular financial adviser, what more is there to say? Just don't do business with him or her, even if he or she is a good friend. If you feel something is wrong, walk away. Always listen to your unconscious mind, as this part of the brain can pick up cues. If you ignore those cues, you will invariably regret it.

    In creating your wealth, choose what you can do and how you will do it. But if you want to achieve your financial goals fast, stand up for what you believe in and what is right. Don't accept second best—ever! Listen to your unconscious mind; be confident, bold, and brave. If you don't get the right signals from the person you are dealing with, don't deal with him or her.

I say all this because I lost money with my first investment when I mixed business with friendship. Never allow friendship to influence an investment decision, because it can be costly. Remember, if you feel uncomfortable about a deal, walk away.

- **Trust your intuition.** I seek advice from my investment adviser and also from friends, but my final decision is also based on my intuition. For instance, based on my intuition and after balancing both the risks and the potential rewards, I started to invest in land. Land investment is hassle-free and incurs minimal maintenance costs. Land can also increase in value fast, if it is strategically located.

   For my investment portfolio, another good investment is residential property. Besides value appreciation and capital growth, residential properties can generate passive income for you—from the rent you received monthly. Mutual funds and unit trusts are also good long-term investments, which in my case give me an average annual return of over 13 percent. Now you can easily invest online and track your investment portfolios using this investment platform: www.fundsupermart.com

   Of course there are many other types of investment that you can include in your investment portfolio. These include bonds, shares or stocks, mutual funds, certificates of deposit, exchange traded funds, money market accounts, commodities such as gold, and derivatives, including options and futures (see appendix B for details.) The types of investment you include in your portfolio depend on your risk appetite. You are the right person to decide what you want to invest in, because it's your money and it's your call.

- **Take responsibility.** Sometimes the trouble is that a person's old behavior can come back fast. For instance, we stop investing 10 percent or more every month from our salary. And when things don't go the way we want, what do we do? We lay blame, right? We blame our family; we blame our expenses; we blame everything except ourselves. When we stop investing that 10 percent, we try to justify. We are smart and fast in coming up with reasons to explain why we should not deduct that amount from our salary. But by playing the blame game, will your financial situation improve? No way!

   The only way you can improve your financial health and create wealth is to take action. Don't blame other people to justify why you are not doing what you are supposed to do. You must take the responsibility and commit to pay yourself every month, and you must also commit to invest that money. Only by doing so will you be able to create your wealth.

   Don't give an excuse that you will start to invest next year, when you received a pay raise. Chances are you won't, because by then you and your family will have more wants that need to be fulfilled.

   Maybe you have said to yourself, *Oh, I know I have to pay myself first* or *Of course I will take responsibility* or *I will invest.* Okay, you know it all, but my question is, have you actually done something about it? For the majority of us, there is a huge gap between what we know and what we do. There is no point in just reading or knowing; you have to take action and responsibility to make things happen. That is why, to be successful, first you must dream about it, and then you must establish your plan. After that you must take action and never give up. Only by doing all these things can you be successful in reaching your goals.

It's Never Too Late to Invest

Some of us may not be categorized as early birds, but it is never too late for anyone to start investing and creating wealth. But remember what I said in the introduction of this book: money doesn't discriminate against anyone. It doesn't care what color or race you are, where you come from, or whether your parents are rich or poor. Money doesn't have eyes to see you or a nose to smell you, so money doesn't discriminate.

Since money doesn't discriminate, anyone—regardless of age or gender—can create wealth. It doesn't matter how difficult the path you have been on. It doesn't matter if you have been in poverty for a long time. It doesn't even matter if you have never achieved a significant degree of success. And it doesn't matter how many times you have failed. All that is required is you must have a strong desire, a plan, and specific knowledge, and you must be committed and willing to work hard. These are the ingredients you need to achieve your goals.

In fact, there is no such thing as too late. I started investing only five years ago, in my mid-forties. Always remember that where there is a will, there is a way. And to become wealthy, as in most endeavors, you must have a will and a strong desire, followed by a plan and by applying proven strategies or methods. Once you have developed a powerful desire and established a plan, your mentality will change. A change in your mentality will set a wheel in motion, and prosperity will come to you. Trust me, this is a universal fact.

So if you have not done anything about your wealth, this is the time to shift your focus from being poor to becoming wealthy. Remember, success begins with a state of mind. You have to dream big! Only by looking and thinking wealthy can you become wealthy. But, of course, don't forget to take action and to work hard.

The Goals Worksheet

The purpose of the Goals Worksheet (GW) is to record and keep track of the types of investment you are involved in (see table on page 64). To fill up the GW, you need to indicate the investment goals you want to achieve. For instance, let's say you want to invest in unit trusts or mutual fund. First, you need to set the target amount of your investment (for example, $60,000). Then you set your target date (for example, three years). Be specific with the day, month, and year. By being specific, you are preparing your mental arsenal to be in sync with your physical effort.

Once these are all set, you know that you have to save $20,000 per year. That target can then be broken into months. By doing so, the target is less intimidating.

By the time the target date comes (the end of three years), you must review to see your progress. Have you achieved your goal, or are you below target? If you are below target, you need to review your strategy and activities to see why you failed to achieve that target. Once you have figured out the problem, fix it so that you can achieve your goal. The important thing to do is act now.

Goals Worksheet

Investment Goals	Target Amount ($)	Target Date	Review/Remarks

Summary

The third strategy of wealth creation is to invest continuously so that your money will reproduce itself and provide a stream of income into your account to create your wealth fast. You must avoid the earn-and-spend cycle at all costs; instead, get yourself into a habit of an earn-and-invest cycle. Remember, money doesn't discriminate against anyone, regardless of age or gender; therefore, it is never too late to invest and start building your wealth now.

Key Takeaways

Think about the things you will take away from strategy 3 and how and when you will implement them.

Topic	Takeaways	Implementation
The Earn-and-Spend Cycle		
The Earn-and-Invest Cycle		
Investment Strategies		
Investment Timing		
Investment Goal Worksheet		

Chapter 6

Strategy 4
Pay Off Your Debt

Some debts are fun when you are acquiring them, but none are fun when you set about retiring them.

Ogden Nash

To live a debt-free life, you need to be able to define your debt problem and to assess it correctly. But this is where the majority of debtors run into trouble, because they don't understand the concept of debt. Although they pay off their debt, it returns shortly afterward. This happened because debtors fail to identify the root cause of debt and therefore open the door to repeating the vicious cycle.

This chapter presents the fourth strategy: paying off your debt. With this strategy come five simple steps to overcome the destructive effects of debt.

Are You Living within Your Means?

I have friends coming to me constantly complaining about not having enough money. From my observation, it wasn't their salary that contributed to their problems, but their ego, habits, and attitudes.

They were constantly living beyond their means. They took loans to finance their wants. For instance, if they wanted a new car or even a new sofa, they took out loans for them. If they wanted new shoes, handbags, designer clothes, or name-brand watches, they charged them on their credit cards. If they saw their neighbors renovating their houses, they wanted to do the same, despite not having the budget. Guess what. They took loans from loan sharks.

How about you? Are you living within your means or burying yourself in debt?

Debt Is Not a Normal Way of Living

Don't be fooled into thinking that debt, especially bad debt, is a normal way of living. Many poor and middle-class people are fooled into believing that debt is a solution to fulfilling their ego and wants. But debt shouldn't even be considered as a normal part of your budget, especially loans taken to finance your wants and to fulfill your ego.

Having much debt is a sign that your budget and financial situation are not healthy. You are, in fact, suffering from a serious disease called *debtbetes*. This disease is more serious than diabetes, as it can destroy the lives of a whole family. You must look at your debt as a sign of the failing health of your finances and be prepared to do anything to get your budget back to good health.

**Don't be fooled into thinking that
debt is a normal part of life.**

Set Yourself Free from Debt

> *Running into debts isn't so bad. It's running into creditors that hurts.*
>
> Unknown

Setting yourself free from debt is easy if you know its root cause. Remember, when you were born, there was no tag attached showing the amount of debt you owed. You were debt-free. When you look at the root cause of all the debts you have, you might be surprised. It has very little to do with your financial problem; it is mostly a personal problem. That may be hard to believe, but it is true.

Your debt is a personal problem disguised as a financial problem. In fact, in most cases, the *real cause of debt is overspending*. And this is all because of personal habits and attitudes. If you can understand and accept that your personal habits and attitudes are the root cause of your debt, you can work hard to overcome them. This is a key, and understanding this principle is what will help you to live a debt-free life.

Unfortunately, failure to understand the root cause of debt is the main reason so many debtors have persistent problems with debt. As a result, they tend to look for different solutions in solving their debt problems.

Five Simple Steps to a Debt-Free Life

Let's take a look at how you can live a debt-free life in five simple steps.

1. **Categorize Your Debt**

   Categorizing your debt is one of the important steps to becoming debt-free. You must be able to differentiate good debt from bad debt. Doing so will help you to come up with a strategy for dealing with different types of debt. Although some financial planners and commentators argue that no debt is good, some debts can be considered good.

   Good Debt

   Let's examine what good debt is. Good debt is an investment that will grow in value and will help to generate income and increase your net worth. Good debt serves a real purpose and fulfills your needs but not your wants. An example of good debt is a mortgage, as it provides a home. (Having a house is not only fulfilling a need but also providing a real purpose in terms of giving you shelter.)

Having rented a house for over two years compared to owning the house, I can say that house debt (a home mortgage) is definitely a good debt. Even though mortgages are long-term loans, they have relatively low monthly payments. This allows you to keep the rest of your money free for other investments. In addition, your house usually increases in value over time. This allows you to cancel out the interest you have paid over that same period. By owning a house, you also have access to equity through refinancing. And the funds can be used to invest in property, shares, or other wealth-building opportunities.

Another example of a good debt is a student loan. This debt helps to raise your income potential, as a college education increases your value as an employee, which can justify the need to borrow the money. But bear in mind that you must limit the amount of money you borrow. Also, only borrow to finance your education and not your car or furniture. I have seen a few students take education loans and use them to finance their weddings. This doesn't make sense at all; they had to quit school because they had nothing left to pay for their education.

Bad Debt

Now let's look at bad debt. This is a debt that doesn't increase your net worth or that is used to purchase goods or services that have no lasting value. A debt is also bad when it is incurred to purchase things that you *want* rather than *need*. One example is credit card spending. It serves only one purpose: to fulfill a want. When you go on a shopping spree with a credit card, you are more likely to buy things you want, not things you need.

The easy money from a credit card that you spend on things you want turns into bad debt when you fail to pay the entire amount you owe. Making only the minimum payments on a high-interest credit card, while continuing to keep balances on the accounts month after month, is an expensive habit that puts you deep into debt. Not many people can quickly recover from credit card debt, and many people have been declared bankrupt because of credit card debt.

According to a 2014 *News Straits Times* report, 1,940 youths in Malaysia below twenty-five years old had been declared bankrupt since 2007. What was more shocking was that 579 out of 1,940 were declared bankrupt in the first six months of 2014. The same report stated that due to reckless spending habits, these youths look at credit cards as an easy way to fulfill their wants so that they can live a lavish lifestyle. In Malaysia, banks require consumers to pay only the minimum, which is 5 percent or RM50 ($14) (whichever is higher) of the outstanding balance.

On top of a high interest rate, you have to pay finance charges if you don't make full payments every month. This means that if you make a partial payment, a minimum payment, or no payment on or before the due date, the bank will impose finance charges from the day the transaction is posted to your card account. Therefore, keeping a balance on a credit card is not a good idea. In fact, Dave Ramsey said, "A credit card balance ringing up 30 percent can turn into a black hole if not paid quickly."

Another example of bad debt is a loan from a loan shark. The term "loan shark" has been commonly used to describe those who lend small sums at higher rates of interest than the law allows. This type of loan is very common among wage earners. The factors that give rise to loan shark transactions are greed among lenders and compelling necessity, shortsightedness, and/or gullibility among borrowers. Many people are in serious trouble because of borrowing from loan sharks. Recently I read about a businessman who is living in fear after a loan shark started to harass him when he failed to pay a loan. So don't become the victim of your own shortsightedness and greed. You must avoid loan sharks at all costs!

Another type of bad debt is a cash advance loan from a credit card or a payday loan similar to a loan from a loan shark. For a payday loan, the borrower writes a personal check to the lender for the amount he wants to borrow, plus a fee. Then he has until his next payday to pay back the loan amount, plus the original fee and any interest incurred over that time period. This is the worst type of debt, because interest rates for payday loans are very high—starting at 300 percent annually. And if the debtor fails to pay back the amount by the next payday, he incurs yet another processing fee to "roll over" the loan.

A car is another example of bad debt. New cars can cost a lot of money. While you may need a vehicle to get yourself to work and to run the errands, paying interest on a car is simply a waste of money. The moment your car leaves the showroom, it is already losing its value. According to Bankrate.com, a car loses between 15 percent and 20 percent of its value each year. A car in its second year will be worth 80 percent to 85 percent of its first-year value, and a car in its third year will be worth 80 percent to 85 percent of its second-year value.

My advice is put your ego aside and pay cash for a used car, if you can afford to do so. If you can't, buy the least expensive reliable vehicle you can find, and pay it off as quickly as you can. Don't allow your ego to add to your financial burdens. Buying expensive cars to show off is not worth it, because spending a large amount of money for something that eventually depreciates is a bad strategy.

Although no one has the right to stop you from buying what you want, that doesn't mean you should put yourself into crippling debt. Unfortunately, many people are living in debt because they can't restrain themselves from buying luxuries that they don't really need or that exceed their income or their ability to pay in a timely manner. The general rule for avoiding bad debt is this: *if you can't afford it and you can survive without it, don't buy it.*

2. Select a Repayment Approach

Once you have categorized your debt, the next step to becoming debt-free is to select a repayment approach. The one you choose will depend on a number of factors. One is the type of debt you have, and the other is the status of your debt-to-income ratio (DTIR).

What is DTIR? It is one way that lenders (including mortgage lenders) measure an individual's ability to manage monthly payment and repay debts. It is calculated by dividing total recurring monthly debt by gross monthly income, and it is expressed as a percentage.

For example, if your DTIR is over 20 percent, it is recommended that you seek the help of a credit counselor to get advice regarding the most effective payment method to pay off your debt. Your counselor will thoroughly review your situation and recommend the strategies that you could implement. For instance, during the counseling session, your counselor might recommend ways for you to cut spending so that you can save some money with which to pay off your debt. I will explain more about DTIR in step 5.

If your debt level is manageable but you are still dealing with multiple nonmortgage debts, you will want to choose the most effective method. The two most popular are the ladder and the debt snowball methods. These methods are explained below.

The ladder method. Think of your debt as a ladder, and you are standing at the top of it. What you want to do is to come down from the ladder as fast as you can and be as efficient as possible so that you don't waste money on unnecessary interest. There are a couple of steps you should take.

First, list each of your debts in order, from largest to smallest interest rate (see example below).

Type of Debt	Amount of Debt ($)	Interest Rate (%)	Minimum Monthly Payment ($)
Account A	350	18	20
Account B	850	13	50
Account C	1000	7	85
Account D	675	5	40
Account E	500	4.5	35
Total	3375		230

Next, set aside money to make the minimum monthly payment for each of the loans. In our hypothetical example, you budgeted about $500 to pay off the debts each month. Since your minimum monthly payment is $230, you have a balance of $270. This balance is then used to pay the account with the highest interest rate: account A, with an interest rate of 18 percent.

Type of Debt	Amount of Debt ($)	Interest Rate (%)	Minimum Monthly Payment ($)
Account A	65.25	18	20
Account B	809.21	13	50
Account C	920.83	7	85
Account D	637.81	5	40
Account E	466.88	4.5	35
Total	2899.98		230

After the first month, account A is almost closed. This is because you will use the balance of $270 to pay off account

A. While you are still paying interest on other debts, you are doing so at a lower percentage than account A, saving you money in the long term.

As you can see, next month you will pay off account A in full. Once you account for interest, you will spend $66.23 on account A and will have a $203.77 surplus to be used to pay off account B. Account B will go from a balance of $809.21 to $767.98 after interest and the minimum payment. But, since you closed account A, you still have a surplus of $203.77, and account B will drop to $564.21. Once you have settled account B, you will target account C and so on.

Basically, when looking at your loan, the principal (the amount before interest) of your debt is not as important as the interest rate. This is because the *interest rate determines how quickly your debt will grow and how much more you will have to pay each month.* By using the ladder method, you minimize the amount of interest paid. This means that you pay less overall.

The debt snowball method. First, list your debts in order from smallest to largest. Ignore interest rates for now, but be sure to include each minimum monthly payment. Here's an example:

Type of Debt	Amount of Debt ($)	Minimum Monthly Payment ($)
Credit Card	500	25
Personal Loan	3000	100
Student Loan	5000	150
Car Loan	20000	430
House Loan	100000	1000
Total	128500	1705

Next, determine how much money you can put toward your debt this month. Let's say you set aside $2,500 in your monthly budget to pay off debt. The total minimum payment for your debt is $1,705, so you have an extra $795 ($2,500 minus $1,705). Put these extra funds of $795 toward the smallest debt, such as your credit card. In this case, the amount you owe in a credit card is $475 ($500 minus $25), and you use the extra funds ($795) to pay off your credit card in full. This is strike one.

After paying your credit card, you still have a balance of $320 ($795 minus $475). This extra fund should be used to pay the next smallest debt, such as your personal loan (minimum monthly payment of $100 plus $320 extra fund) to further reduce the amount to $2,480 ($2,900 minus $420).

Once you understand the debt snowball method, you will see just how quickly your surplus can grow as your total minimum monthly payment decreases from $1,705 to $1,680. Take a look at the table below.

Type of Debt	Amount of Debt ($)	Minimum Monthly Payment ($)
Credit Card	0	Settled!
Personal Loan	2580	100
Student Loan	4850	150
Car Loan	19570	430
House Loan	99000	1000
Total	**126000**	**1680**

After just one month of debt repayment, your minimum monthly payment total drops to $1,680 as you have settled the credit card debt. And the good news is your surplus grows to

$820 ($2,500 minus $1,680). With the surplus of $820 plus the minimum monthly payment of $100 ($920), after the second month, your personal loan will be further reduced to $1,660 ($2,580 minus $920), and soon this loan will be settled too.

Now that you know how to pay off debt with the debt snowball method, you probably see how quickly this method produces results. Imagine how much more convenient life will be when you are making fewer debt payments each month. And the most rewarding part is you will have more money in your pocket.

3. Be Organized

To achieve significant success in life, it is important to be organized. Research shows that the majority of successful people are organized. We all know the reasons why getting rid of the mess and better managing our time and life are important. This is because if we don't, we are adding unnecessary stress to our life.

Remember the last time you were late to an important meeting or job interview because you couldn't find your car keys? Do you realize what happened? Your stress level peaked and possibly your blood pressure also elevated. Your body started to tense up, and then you became irritable. When you fail to organize yourself, your mind feels muddled and confused, and you are more likely to give up on any task you undertake.

In dealing with your debt repayment, it is important to get organized. To get organized, make a visual representation of all your debts. On page 78 is an Excel sheet called Debt Payoff Table (DPT) for recording the details of your debts.

Debt Payoff Table

No.	Creditor	Amount Owed ($)	Duration	Minimum Monthly Payment ($)	Monthly Interest Amount ($)	Interest Rate	Monthly Due Date
	Total						

There are at least five reasons why the DPT is important. First, it allows you to consolidate all your debts in one sheet, making it easy for your reference.

Second, showing the amount owed, duration of the debts, minimum monthly payments, interest rates, due date, and total balances all on one sheet makes it easier for you to decide which payment method you will use to pay your debts.

Third, as you adjust the amount and the balance each month, the DPT helps you see your progress and gives you the motivation you need.

Fourth, it gives you a visual representation of where you stand. And when you have a constant visual reminder, you are more likely to be committed to pay off the debts. Remember, seeing is believing!

Finally, the DPT functions as a dashboard to help you keep track of your repayment progress each month. This is important because you want to get as much encouragement and motivation as possible, because your goal is to become debt-free.

4. Form New Habits and Stick to Them

People who are successful in their business, love life, health, or finances are that way because they have formed new habits. But they have paid a high price too, because developing new habits requires hard work and sacrifice. And once they formed new habits, they stuck to them.

Sticking to your new habits is important for two reasons. First, you don't want all the effort you put in to become just quick fixes, instead of solving your problems in the long-term. Second, you don't want the new habits to be temporary, so that you fall back into your old habits.

How do you make sure you will stick to your new habits? You must attach rewards to them, because rewards provide motivation and encouragement. Your reward might be financial freedom and a new lifestyle that is free from debt. In fact, it is much easier to stick to a new habit if you can anticipate a reward at a later date.

How to Form New Habits

All habits are different, and some are easier to form than others. In my experience, forming a new habit to pay off debts when they are due is not easy when you are financially tight. But this should not be an excuse for not settling your debts on time and getting your life back on track. The following three simple steps can help you to do it.

A. Form small habits. Stanford University researcher, B. J. Fogg suggested that we focus on forming "small habits," as minor habits and behaviors matter. According to Fogg, a small habit

- is a behavior you do at least once a day;
- takes you less than thirty seconds to do;

- requires little effort; and
- is relevant to the full behavior.

To form a small habit for saving, I suggest that every time you come back from work, deposit ten dollars into a piggy bank. Do this every day, five days a week, and four weeks a month.

- Do it immediately once you reach home. (It takes less than thirty seconds to do.)
- Ensure that you put that money into the designated piggy bank. (This requires little effort if you have allocated a piggy bank for that purpose.)
- At the end of the month, total how much you have saved.

This small behavior will motivate you, which will make it easier for you to save *more than* ten dollars a day. Once you have cultivated the small habits, bigger habits will be easier to form. That's because your behavior is changed due to constant practice, and you can see the results of your new habit.

B. Do a small habit immediately after an existing habit.
Identify an existing habit. Ask yourself, "What behavior do I always do, regardless of how I feel?" This may include impulsive spending and using credit card instead of cash. Find a corrective action that will come after you do that thing out of habit.

For example, if you frequently use a credit card for your purchases (existing behavior), you must pay the amount you owe in full (corrective action). I can't emphasize how important it is to do the corrective action immediately after you realize your behavior. This has created a fear in me about using credit cards for shopping, because I know I will have to pay the outstanding balance in full. This small habit has been partly responsible for my financial success.

C. Celebrate your success. The final step in forming a small habit is to celebrate your success. Celebrating helps keep you on track and motivates you to achieve your goals. Although it is important to stay on course to make sure you reach your goals, don't forget to enjoy the ride. Be sure to stop and smell the roses.

When I formed a small habit, such as paying myself more than 10 percent a month, I celebrated my success by inviting my family to dinner at a popular seafood restaurant and taking them on an overseas vacation. Looking at the smiling faces around the dinner table and seeing them experience new places gave me the motivation to create more new habits. In fact, there are multiple ways you can celebrate your successes. Once you have paid off all your debts and your savings have ballooned, you can treat your family to a holiday. Why not? You need to celebrate your success. But whatever you do, do it within your budget.

5. Assess Your Situation and Know Your Limits

This is the final step to becoming debt-free. Too many people get deep into debt because they don't understand how credit works. As I already mentioned, debt is not a financial problem. It is a personal problem disguised as a financial problem due to lack of understanding. Once you get into debt, it's very hard to get out. But it is not the end of the world; you can still get out of debt, provided you understand how credit works.

Among the most important things for you to do is to evaluate your situation so that you know the limit of your debt. This can be done by calculating your debt-to-income ratio (DTIR). As I mentioned earlier, your DTIR is calculated by dividing your total recurring monthly debt by your gross monthly income, and it is expressed as a percentage, as shown below.

$$\text{DTIR} = \frac{\text{Total Debt}}{\text{Total Income}} \times 100$$

As an example, to calculate your DTIR, add up all your monthly debt payments and divide them by your gross monthly income. Your gross monthly income is generally the amount of money you have earned before your taxes and other deductions are taken out. For example, if you pay $1,500 a month for your mortgage and another $700 a month for an auto loan and $600 a month for the rest of your debts, your monthly debt payments are $2,800 ($1,500 plus $700 plus $600). If your gross monthly income is $6,000, your DTIR is 46 percent ($2,800 divided by $6,000 times 100).

At a minimum, it is recommended that your DTIR stay below 20 percent for nonmortgage debt. Ideally, it is better to stay at 15 percent or below. Once you incorporate a mortgage into the figure, it is recommended that you keep your total DTIR at or below 36 percent. Evidence from studies of mortgage loans suggests that borrowers with a higher DTIR are more likely to run into trouble making monthly payments.

When you take into account your age, the following are guidelines for nonmortgage debt:

- If you are under thirty-five years of age and your DTIR is below 15 percent, you are fine. But if your DTIR is above 15 percent, you are already in the danger zone.
- If you are between thirty-five and fifty-five, and you are the sole wage earner, you are fine if your DTIR is below 10 percent. But if your DTIR is above 10 percent, you are in the danger zone.

- If you are between thirty-five and fifty-five, and you and your spouse are wage earners, you are fine provided your DTIR is below 15 percent. However, if your DTIR is above 15 percent, you are already in the danger zone.
- If you are over fifty-five, and your DTIR is under 10 percent, you are fine. But if your DTIR is above 10 percent, you are in the danger zone.

You also need to take note that even if this indicator shows that you are fine, it is more likely that you will be in trouble if one or more of the following situations applies to you:

- You are unable to save money because of your debt payments.
- You depend on other sources of income to pay your expenses.
- You rely on credit cards for your purchases.
- You make only the minimum monthly payments on your debts.
- You borrow from one lender to pay another or use one credit card to pay another.
- You borrowed from a friend or relative, or you take an advance at work to pay your bills.
- You make late payments on most of your bills or miss paying your bills on some months.
- Creditors or debt collection agencies are running after you.

Know the Rules

As a general rule, if you are spending more than 28 percent of your income to pay your mortgage or more than 36 percent of your income to pay your total loans, you are seriously overburdened with debt. On page 84 are the guidelines you can use to assess your situation.

Type of Debt	What It Includes	What Is the Threshold
Consumer	Non-mortgage obligations, including auto loans, credit cards, personal loans, student loans, etc.	20 percent of your monthly net income
Mortgage	Mortgage payment, home insurance, property taxes, etc.	28 percent of your monthly gross income
Total	Both consumer debts and mortgage debts	36 percent *or less* of your monthly gross income

Let's assess your situation based on the above guidelines. Assume that your gross monthly income is $6,000 and net income is $5,700. You just bought a house, and now you want to furnish it. To do that, you decide to use a credit card. You are also thinking of buying a new car, and you take out a loan to finance it. After a few months, you start to worry as your debts starts to eat up a big chunk of your income. Assume your total monthly payment for your consumer loan is $1,606, and your total monthly repayment for the mortgage is $1,586.

Based on the assessment (see the table below), you found out that although your mortgage debt (26 percent) is not exceeding the recommended limit (28 percent), it's obvious that your consumer (28 percent) and total debts (53 percent) far exceed the recommended limit (20 percent and 36 percent, respectively). It is obvious that you are seriously overburdened with debt.

Type of Debt	Recommended Limit	Your Repayment Position	Exceed Threshold?
Consumer	(20 percent x $5700 = $1140)	Monthly payment of $1606 or 28 percent	Yes
Mortgage	(28 percent x $6000 = $1680)	Monthly payment of $1586 or 26 percent	No
Total	(36 percent x $6000 = $2160)	Monthly payment of $3192 or 53 percent	Yes

Doing this assessment and having these facts can help you make the right decisions regarding your financial health. Hence, it is important to make assessments of your financial obligations so that you know your limit and are able to take corrective action.

Summary

It is important to remember that the debts you have accumulated are (probably) due to personal rather than financial problems. Most people accumulate debt due to overspending to fulfill their wants rather than controlled spending to meet their needs. This happens because of personal habits and attitudes.

No one ever said that paying back debt was easy, but when you understand the concept of debt and credit, and with a positive mind-set and the right payment method that you choose, you can get out of debt and become financially healthy.

Key Takeaways

Think about the things you will take away from strategy 4 and how and when you will implement them.

Topic	Takeaways	Implementation
Living within Your Means		
The Root Cause of Your Debt		
Categorize Your Debt		
Methods to Settle Your Debt		
Form New Habits		
Analyze and Determine Your DTIR		

Chapter 7

Strategy 5
Protect Your Wealth

Wealth can only be accumulated by the earnings of industry and the savings of frugality.

John Tyler

The majority of people focus on growing their wealth, but protecting wealth is just as important. George S. Clason states in his book *The Richest Man in Babylon*, "Gold in a man's purse must be guarded with firmness, else it be lost." There is no point in working hard to accumulate wealth if you can't protect it. You must protect your wealth just as you protect your children.

This chapter presents the fifth strategy: protecting your wealth. There are rules that you have to follow to ensure your wealth is protected. However, before I discuss those rules, it is crucial to know why protecting your wealth is important:

- Building your wealth is not easy. It needs your effort to establish a plan and it needs your hard work, discipline, commitment, and, above all, your sacrifices to execute a plan to achieve your financial goals.
- It also needs specific knowledge and skill. These come through learning and training, which require spending some money.
- Building your wealth requires valuable time and lots of patience over long periods.
- Building your wealth requires the very valuable ingredient: money.
- It is important to protect your wealth, because an unexpected event, such as an accident or illness, can happen in a blink of an eye, and you could lose your wealth. I don't think you want

to lose your wealth after working so hard and for so long to accumulate it.

How to Protect Your Wealth

It is important to protect your wealth from changes in your personal situation, such as illness, accident, injury, and even death, because these events can cause your wealth to erode, both during your lifetime and after you are gone. Although it might sound cruel, it is also important to protect your wealth from friends, relatives, and even family members. Also protect your wealth from investors you hardly know or ones you think you may know. Often investors are eager to invite you to invest in business ventures by promising you huge returns. But keep in mind that the first sound principle of investment is security for the capital you invest. Don't be easily enticed by the promise of huge returns. Always study a proposal carefully before you decide to part with your money. Also seek the advice of experts. Remember, don't be misled by empty promises, because genuine ways to create wealth take time, effort, knowledge, lots of patience, and sacrifice.

To stay wealthy, you must protect your wealth.

Here are four simple rules to follow in protecting your wealth.

- **Don't Be Greedy**

  Once you start accumulating wealth, don't be greedy. If you are greedy, you will tend to invest without good judgment. In an article on the InvestingAnswers website, Sean Quinn admitted that he went from billionaire to bankruptcy due to greed. Quinn, who was worth $6 billion in 2008, according to Forbes, owed Anglo Irish Bank $2.7 billion and was declared bankrupt. So the lesson learned is to be careful not to become greedy in your own quest for wealth.

  I have a friend who lost $1 million investing in a business that promised a return of 10 percent per month. He was paid for only four months before the "business owners" disappeared. Remember, if it is too good to be true, it probably is. So be suspicious of people or situations that offer a large benefit for very little. There is just no way to get huge benefits for doing nothing.

  Most wealthy people agree that accumulating money can be highly motivating, but when it becomes an obsession, the results can be disastrous. Remember back in 2008, during the major market crash? Many companies closed down, and many people lost a significant portion of their life savings. Some countries nearly became insolvent. And many greedy investors lost their savings and properties; some were even on the run to avoid the authorities.

  I have friends who not only were out of a job, but were also out of money as a result of losing their wealth in the stock market. So don't be greedy, because greed can bring financial disaster.

- **Work with People You Trust**

  This is a simple rule, but many people ignore it. If you want to stay wealthy, make sure you can trust people you do business with—even if they are friends, relatives, and family members. There is no point in doing business with people you don't trust. Always remind yourself that if you feel something is wrong, it's time to walk away. Don't feel bad or feel obligated to make a deal.

Listen to your heart. If you ignore the clues, you will invariably regret it. I have experienced this before: I ignored the clue and lost out. So my advice to you is to deal with the people you really trust and to make sure you have the agreement in writing.

- **Know When to Say No**

To protect your wealth, you need to know when to say no. If you keep saying yes, you can get into serious trouble. Remember, when you are nobody and you don't have money, no one cares about you. But once you have money, many people will call you their best friend, brother, or even daddy. It sounds ridiculous, but it is true! They see you as an easy target, especially when you are generous. They also see you as owing them something, just because both of you went to the same school, for example. In their mind, it is worth it for them to take a chance on you.

When they hear of your kindness, they will want to borrow money from you, because they know you might be the source of a low-interest or even free loan. They know that it isn't easy to borrow from financial institutions. But it is important to remind yourself that you are not a bank, nor are you a charitable organization.

A few people borrowed money from me—and none of them paid me back. It was not only frustrating to keep sending reminders to them (which they ignored), but I also felt used by them. Last year, a friend promised to pay me the amount he owed me, but even he ignores my phone calls or messages. So it is better to say no when people want to borrow money from you than to feel frustrated and used.

But how do you say no to friends, relatives, and family members who want to borrow money from you? This is easy if you have a policy of not lending money. You need to make it very clear to them that you are not a bank. Hopefully they will understand and will never ask again. If a family member insists, and he or she becomes offended, take it as a red flag that it would *definitely* be unwise to lend to him or her.

What about lending to loved ones? This is also a bad idea, because it puts your relationship in jeopardy. Trust me, doing so will jeopardize the relationship. So to maintain healthy relationships, don't do it. When someone you love is in serious need, and you have the means to help, there are two things you can do. First, set up the terms and a schedule for repayment with your loved ones, and make sure both parties are in agreement. By doing so, your money stays protected and your relationship is not jeopardized. Second, if you decided to lend the money on good faith, don't expect to be paid back.

One piece of advice: you have all the right to say either yes or no, because it is your money, and you can do whatever you want with it. When it comes to dealing with money, use your head, not your heart.

• **Buy Insurance**

Most of us insure our car and home but not what is most important: our life and our ability to earn an income. Remember, in your quest for wealth creation, your most valuable asset is your ability to earn an income; after all, this is what keeps money coming. Also keep in mind that wealth protection is the foundation of any strong financial plan. The protection you get minimizes the impact of events outside your control.

One such protection is life insurance, which preserve your family's lifestyle in the event of you being disabled, having a seriously illness, or dying. Determining the right amount of protection is ultimately a question of balance. You need to ask yourself what stage of your wealth creation life cycle you are in. How would you cope if your spouse became critically ill? How would your spouse and dependents cope if you became critically ill?

What assets do you have to support your lifestyle? How many dependents do you have, and are your children still in school? And what lifestyle options are you protecting? All these questions are important in deciding the types and amount of insurance you need. Hence, it is very important for you to talk to your wealth management adviser and seek his or her advice so that you are well protected.

Summary

To stay wealthy, you must protect your wealth from loss. Loss can be avoided by not lending money to friends, relatives, or even immediate family members, because you might not get your money back, and it could jeopardize the relationship. In fact, money can be a serious force in driving apart friends and family members. Therefore, trust your instincts, and simply decline to lend the money if you feel uneasy about the deal.

And before you decide to invest your money, make sure you consult experts, because their experience and knowledge can protect you from making unsafe investments. Always remember to ensure the security of your investment. Invest only in a portfolio that gives you some assurance of returns.

Key Takeaways

Think about the things you will take away from strategy 5 and how and when you will implement them.

Topic	Takeaways	Implementation
Why Protecting Your Wealth Is Important		
Who to Protect Your Wealth From		
How to Protect Your Wealth		

Chapter 8

Strategy 6
Insure Your Future Income

I'd like to live as a poor man with lots of money.

Pablo Picasso

Today you may be wealthy, but tomorrow you could be living on the street. Today you can have all the strength to build your wealth, but in a few years you may not have it anymore, because every day we are growing old. Remember, nothing is certain except dying. This is fact of life, and no one can deviate from it. You also never know when God will call you. The only thing you can do is prepare.

I still remember the Asian financial crisis that gripped much of South East Asia in 1997. Countries like Malaysia, Indonesia, South Korea, Thailand, Laos, Hong Kong, and the Philippines were badly affected by the slump. Before the financial crisis, many of my friends were wealthy, managing their own businesses as securities brokers. They were enjoying their wealth and had bought expensive homes and fleets of cars, and they went for exotic holidays. They enjoyed the life of the rich and famous.

One day I called my broker friend because I wanted to buy shares. He never answered my call, and I found out from another broker that I was not worth his time. I felt sad, but that was the truth. I was told that most of the brokers were dealing only with wealthy clients, and I was not one of them.

But as they were so busy making money and enjoying material wealth, they were caught off-guard when the market crashed. All of them went out of business and lost their expensive homes, cars—everything they had worked hard for. Some were on the run, because banks and debt collection agencies were running after them. It was tragic! Why was it happening to those securities brokers?

This chapter presents the sixth strategy of wealth creation: insuring your future income. Don't ignore this strategy, because there is no point in working hard to accumulate wealth, only to see it disappear right before your eyes.

Why Insure Your Future Income?

One day I came back from school soaking wet, and I remembered my father had told me not to forget to bring an umbrella, regardless of the weather conditions. This advice is also applicable when it comes to preparing for our financial future. We must always be prepared, as we never know what will come our way financially. Here are seven reasons why you must insure your future income.

- **Old age.** Whether we like it or not, most of us will grow old one day, and some of us will leave this world before we get old. Don't ignore this, as this is the path of our life, and no one can escape from it. Regardless of what happens, we must make a plan to ensure that future income keeps coming to sustain our lives or the lives of loved ones who are left behind. Failure to do so can result in tragedy, as many experienced during the Asian financial crisis in 1997. Unfortunately, many people fail to plan for a rainy day comes without warning. Few young people think that they will become old, and even some adults think they will be young forever. But you must remember that old age comes quickly, often without us realizing it. Therefore, you must seize every opportunity not only to make money, but also to ensure that money will come in during your golden days.

- **Circumstances change.** We can't avoid accidents and illness. We also can't avoid acts of God, such as tsunamis, floods, and earthquakes. According to the World Bank, the total damage caused by the Aceh tsunami was $4.45 billion, almost equal to Aceh's GDP in 2003. Although you can't avoid acts of God, if you plan accordingly, you can minimize the devastating consequences you and your family could face. So remember to insure your future income, as you can't predict what will happen tomorrow.

- **Don't rely on your children.** Many parents rely too much on their children, believing that their children owe them. In Asian culture, it has almost become a tradition that children take care of their aging parents. I am not against tradition or culture or belief, but I have seen many aging parents depend too much on their children for survival. I am not saying that you shouldn't ask for help from your children or that your children should not be willing to help you, but, in most cases, children have their own obligations and commitments. They have children of their own, and they have debts and other financial obligations that drain their finances. Remember that the cost of living during your children's time will probably be much higher than yours is even now. And don't be surprised if they need your help. So plan your finances wisely to avoid becoming a scrounger during your golden days.

- **You can't rely on the state.** Life now is more difficult than it was ten or fifteen years ago. Goods, services, and property are becoming more expensive. I remember when I bought my lovely semidetached house eleven years ago; it cost $90,000. Now a much smaller house costs about $200,000. If you think that the state will come to your rescue when you need it, you can forget about it. Many countries are on the verge of bankrupt; most countries are surviving on debt. According to DaveManuel.com, as of May 4, 2016, the outstanding public debt of the United States was $19,170,001,895,674. It was reported that every man, woman, and child in the United States owes $63,096 for their share of the US public debt. So don't rely on the state; be prepared to survive on your own. The way to do that is to prepare yourself financially now. Invest now so that you will be able to harvest later.

- **The economy.** We can't deny that life is becoming tougher as most countries are facing tough economic situations. Unemployment rates are high while goods are becoming more expensive. The cost of medical care is skyrocketing compared to ten years ago. The overall cost of living is on the rise while high-paying jobs are becoming scarcer. Imagine getting closer to retirement and realizing you can't cover all your expenses, especially medical bills. How would you feel?

  You may be busy putting your children through college, paying your debts, and even supporting your aging parents, but don't ignore your future. As you focus on immediate financial issues, it's easy to overlook the importance of insuring your future income. But if you ignore it, you can be in big trouble. Therefore, start planning your financial future now. Always remember, the earlier you start to prepare for your financial future, the better, and the less stress you will feel. You don't want to be under extreme stress when you are in your golden years, because that is the time to enjoy your grandchildren.

- **The importance of financial freedom.** Since you have been working so hard to accumulate wealth and to enjoy the freedom money can bring, it is just not right for you to lose control of your financial freedom. Can you imagine what it was like for the wealthy securities brokers mentioned in the beginning of the chapter, who lost everything in the blink of an eye, including their dignity and reputation. This happened to them because they ignored the importance of financial freedom. If you ignore this principle, you will not be prepared for a rainy day; you will have a tendency to fulfill your wants now rather than anticipate and prepare for your needs later in life. So don't ignore the importance of your future financial freedom, and be prepared.

- **Enjoy life.** Life is not all about working, and few of us want to be working hard when we are old. Even if you want to keep working, not many employers will want to employ you.

I have seen so many people work until they die, without ever enjoying life. I don't think you want to be like them—working until you are very old and then suddenly dying. It is not worth it. There is more to life than work, and when you have accumulated wealth, you should take time to enjoy it. Remember, wealthy people buy luxuries last. So this is the time for you to enjoy your wealth.

How to Prepare for a Future Income

Here are five simple strategies to ensure that your income keeps flowing in.

- **Buy property.** When you buy a property, such as a residential or commercial building, you can potentially profit through rental yields and capital gains. In fact, rental income from property is a very popular type of passive income. You can also sell your property for more than you initially paid for it. When you buy residential property, always remember that location is among the most important criteria. A strategic location will make it easy to get tenants. And always consider buying property that is not far from where you live, as tenants may need you at any time. Imagine buying a residential property and having to drive many hours or even take a flight to reach your property. This costs not only money but also time that you don't have. Therefore, always buy property within reach.

- **Buy land.** Land almost always appreciates in value. In the event that you need cash, you can sell your land. When I bought land, I always engaged reliable and trusted agents. Once I get a price quote from the real estate agent, I have two options: to contact a certified assessor to give me the valuation of the land that I intend to purchase, and to ask the bank to do a valuation of the land. (If I have to take a bank loan, I negotiate with the bank regarding the valuation fees—for example, either the bank pays the fee for me, or I pay 50 percent). I buy land only if its value is higher than the seller's asking price; this means I make money instantly. Many people I know receive good rental income on their land every month, such as to telecommunications companies. I have also seen landowners make their fortune by developing their land into commercial or residential estates through joint ventures with property developers. So buying land is a good way to ensure the flow of future income.

- **Buy shares.** There is no harm in buying shares, and many people I know have gained substantial wealth dealing in shares. But remember, invest only in shares that you know and understand, and always seek professional help. Since most of us don't have time to understand the share market, since it can be quite complicated, it is worth getting information from a trusted broker. Don't be a jack-of-all-trades and master of none.

- **Invest.** Keep investing, and when you do it, always pursue high interest rates, so that the money you invest can be optimized. And don't forget to diversify to maximize your return; investing in different portfolios rather than just one, because doing so will help you get the best returns. Although diversification doesn't guarantee against loss, it is one of the important components of reaching long-range financial goals while minimizing risk. You can also invest in promising startups, as many people have made their wealth that way. But first do your homework thoroughly. Remember, investing is the Holy Grail to becoming a millionaire, so make your money work hard for you.

- **Insurance.** Never ignore insurance. You must get sizeable insurance policies to help protect yourself and your loved ones in the event of unforeseen circumstances. Like my father said, "Never forget to bring your umbrella, regardless of the weather conditions." Always be prepared, as you don't want to close the barn door after the horse has bolted.

Summary

My advice is never to assume tomorrow will be the same, because it will not. Ensure your future income so that your lifestyle is not interrupted. To do this, I recommended these simple strategies: buy property, land, and shares; keep investing and diversifying; and buy insurance. If you do this, your retirement years will be secure and enjoyable. Don't gamble with your life and the lives of your loved ones. Get your umbrella ready even when the sun is shining!

Key Takeaways

Think about the things you will take away from strategy 6 and how and when you will implement them.

Topic	Takeaways	Implementation
Why Insure Your Future Income?		
How to Prepare for a Future Income		

Chapter 9

Strategy 7
Increase Your Ability to Earn More

Invest in yourself. Your career is the engine of your wealth.
Paul Clitheroe

Throughout my professional and speaking career, I've met many highly qualified and talented employees. However, the problem with some of them is they constantly complain about not having enough money. Some of them wish their salary would increase, and some wish for a promotion. Unfortunately, nothing will happen to us if all we do is wish.

This chapter presents the final strategy: increase your ability to earn more. This is one of the most vital ways to become wealthy. As an employee, you will never be able to become wealthy if you earn less but spend more. You must do the opposite: earn more and spend less. This chapter also discusses five reasons why some employees fail to increase their earnings and includes seven ways to increase your earning ability.

The Difference between the Rich and the Poor

In wealth creation endeavors, there are two groups of employees. One is rich, while the other is poor. Those in the rich group have the power to increase their earning ability because they have definite, strong, and specific desires to do so. As a result, they enjoy the following outcomes:

- a positive and promising life
- tangible results
- a wealthy lifestyle and financial freedom

Those in the poor group have weak and general desires, which are wishes. Because they have only a wish list, they experience the following outcomes:

- a negative and frustrating life
- intangible results
- deep indebtedness and continuous financial difficulties

Rich people's minds vs. poor people's minds

See below the difference between rich people's mental accounts and those of poor people's.

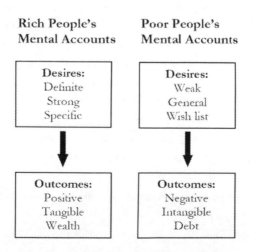

When You Fail to Increase Your Earning Ability

There are a number of reasons why employees fail to increase their earning ability. The first is a lack of definite, specific, and strong desires. George S. Clason wrote in his book *The Richest Man in Babylon*, "Preceding accomplishment must be desire. Thy desires must be strong and definite. General desires are but weak longings. For a man to wish to be rich is of little purpose. For a man to desire five pieces of gold is a tangible desire which he can press to fulfillment."

To put it another way, if you just wish to earn more, it is of little purpose. You must have a definite, specific, and strong desire. For example, you want to increase your income from $40,000 to $200,000 a year. That desire is a powerful motivational force that makes you more creative in looking for ways to increase your earning ability.

When you have definite, specific, and strong desires, you can push yourself beyond limits. You can think outside the box. You can feel that suddenly you have more energy and strength to pursue your dreams. And you despise wasting time, because you have specific goals to achieve within a specified time.

On the other hand, if your desire is general and weak (for example, you want to be rich), you will never have the strength and energy to pursue your dreams and goals, because you don't believe you can achieve them. Remember, we can achieve anything if we believe in it. I am not merely saying this because I want to; I know that everything I have achieved was the result of my belief and, of course, hard work. When I believe that I can achieve a goal I set, the power of belief paves the way and gives me the strength I need to go for my goals. So far I have never failed to achieve my goals.

The second reason employees fail to increase their earning ability is a lack of the skills and knowledge necessary to work at a higher level or to take greater responsibilities. What I mean by *skills* here are people skills, communication skills, leadership skills, negotiation skills, and presentation skills. Once your employer realizes that you don't have the necessary skills and knowledge, it will be very difficult for you to move up the ladder.

The third reason is failure to take ownership. If you want to move ahead in your career, you must take ownership of it. This means you must be willing to develop abilities, knowledge, and skills that are valued by your employer. It is your responsibility to engage in continuous self-improvement, because doing so will equip you with the knowledge and skills needed for your job. By learning more, you prepare yourself to earn more.

The fourth reason is inadequate qualifications. In the current competitive business environment, qualifications are important gauges of how well an employee can perform on a job. If you don't believe me, try to hire employees with prior training and experience, but with minimal qualifications. Then promote them to senior positions. They will likely perform poorly because they do not have the training, background, or knowledge needed to perform the higher-level job, which requires strategic and analytical thinking.

The fifth reason is staying too long with one employer. Nowadays, most people change jobs often for better opportunities, such as a higher salary and more benefits. I am not saying to job hop, but do not stagnate and get frustrated. Once you are frustrated, your productivity will decrease, and your employer will see that. The end result: you will not be promoted, which means you will not be able to increase your income.

Seven Ways to Increase Your Earning Ability

Here are seven ways to increase the value of your best asset—that is, *you*—so that you can increase your earning ability.

- **Excellent communication skills.** The importance of effective communication for employees and managers cannot be overemphasized. Everything done in the workplace involves communication. This is especially important as business transactions increasingly turn global. Both managers and employees must know how to communicate effectively with the company's international counterparts. Differences in culture require managers to understand terms commonly used in one culture that another culture finds offensive.

Good communication is needed to increase efficiency, satisfy customers, improve quality, and create innovative products. Few employees rise through the corporate ranks without good communication skills. Studies show that these skills can give you an edge in getting better jobs and can help you move up the ladder to better-paying positions.

In reality, communication skills not only help you get the job you want, they also help you to be more successful in the job you have. Take a minute to think about people you know who have been very effective in their work and in their relationships. Chances are they know how to use communication skills to get their ideas across, to advance their missions, to engage others, and to enlist people's support.

If these skills aren't your best, sharpen them. Here are few ways to do that.

➢ Strike up conversations with a colleague, and exchange ideas.
➢ Read good books. This helps you boost your vocabulary and articulate your thoughts more clearly.
➢ Be a good listener. When you have a conversation with a colleague, be intentional about listening to what he or she says instead of thinking about what you are going to say next. Remember, you were born with one mouth and two ears, so talk once and listen twice.

- **Enhance your credentials.** If you have credentials, don't keep them inside your drawer. Use them. You need to be proud of your credentials because they represent measurable accomplishments in your career, including your degrees and awards you have won. Remember, credentials give you credibility.

With credibility, you will have an advantage as in getting a better job. However, if you think your credentials are not so promising because you don't have a formal education, you need to work hard to get one. Nowadays it is fairly easy and not too expensive to earn a degree or get professional qualification through evening or part-time classes. Research shows that formal education can prepare you for higher-level jobs, and it does impact income. In fact, according to billionaire Warren Buffet, "The more you learn, the more you'll earn."

Studies also reveal that even if you are an established entrepreneur with a great reputation, clients and potential business partners are still looking at qualifications. The more qualified you are, the more business you will likely attract. Remember, it is worth enhancing your credentials.

- **Be an expert.** As the working environment becomes more internationalized and increasingly competitive, employees need to be competent and knowledgeable. Pat Riley said in his book *The Winner Within*, "If you are not committed to getting better at what you are doing, you are bound to get worse." This is true, because anything less than a commitment to excellent performance is an unconscious acceptance of mediocrity.

  One way to earn more is to become an expert or specialist. An expert is a person who has achieved high visibility and also created a distinguishable personal brand and credibility within an industry. The key to becoming an expert is to know how to go from having a cluttered mind to having specialized knowledge. One way to become an expert is to educate yourself continually. This doesn't have to be traditional education. You can acquire knowledge and expertise by attending seminars, reading books, listening to tapes, or attending conferences.

  Did you know that the average person reads only one or two books a year? If you want to be an expert, read at least two books that pertain to your field each month. At the end of a couple of years, you will be an expert in your field. If you want to increase your ability to earn more, becoming an expert is one of the ways. However, you must focus your efforts to becoming great at what you do.

I once read about a reputable oil and gas company looking for a drilling specialist and offering a salary of $61,200 per month. So do you think it is worth it to become an expert?

- **Increase your ability to apply knowledge and skills.** Having skills and knowledge to offer to your employer will definitely increase your earning ability. In fact, Brian Tracy says in his book *The Power of Self Confidence*, "Your ability to earn money by applying your knowledge and skill is the most important single source of money in your life." He called this "earning power" because it is your ability to get results that someone will pay you for. And this is absolutely true, especially when the business world is so competitive and most companies are scaling back and cutting overhead costs.

    "Time on the job" now doesn't matter as much as "results on the job," and most companies keep only a skeleton crew of specialists essential to the business; they eliminate those who are not skillful and productive. In fact, most employers nowadays have been scrambling to find new pay systems that pay for performance.

    If you are a knowledgeable and skillful employee so a company can benefit from you, you can increase your earning ability. If you just sell your loyalty to the company, be ready to be laid off, because results are the commodity that most employers want.

    Be ready to repackage your talents, skills, and results so you can sell them to your employer or prospective employers. If you think your skills are not current, you must educate yourself either through formal or informal education. I earned my PhD fifteen years ago, and I keep updating my knowledge and skills by continually educating myself both formally and informally. You should be doing the same if you want to become the hot commodity employers want.

- **Invest in yourself.** The best investment you can make is an investment in yourself. You can do this by continually improving your skills, knowledge, talents, and experience in a specific area or areas that will give you the best lifelong earning potential.

In fact, by investing in yourself, such as taking advanced degrees or specialized courses, you are turning yourself into valuable human capital. You are also delivering value to your employer, and that is what the employer wants to pay you for.

A continuous investment in yourself will also make you more confident, which is important for your self-esteem. The more confident you are, the better your chances of increasing your earning ability, because you can prove to your employer that you are not only competent, but also able to take on additional responsibility. And by continuously investing in yourself, you will eventually achieve competency and mastery in your chosen field.

- **Be indispensable.** Since good employees are always in demand, being viewed as an indispensable worker will not only improve the likelihood of your advancement within the organization but also increase your earnings.

  Seth Godin, in his book *Linchpin*, states, "The indispensable employee brings humanity and connection and art to their organization. They are the key player, the one who's difficult to live without, the person you can build something around."

  Becoming an indispensable employee requires the mastery of your tasks and the continual development of your professional skills. So be willing to invest in yourself and to make yourself an indispensable employee.

- **Improve your visibility.** Make yourself visible and get noticed. You can make decision makers aware of your accomplishments and expertise without overtly blowing your horn. Take on a difficult project to show the decision makers your talent and capability. Or ask your manager for chances to work on different assignments or on cross-functional teams, an experience that will allow you to get to know colleagues and professionals in different parts of your organization.

Improving your visibility essentially means effective internal networking. The more people know about your talent, the better opportunity you will have. Don't underestimate the power of visibility. And, most importantly, don't underestimate your own capability to be visible; you have it, but you fail to realize it. Remember, all of us were born special, and all of us have the capability to be visible. Let yourself shine now!

Summary

Increasing your ability to earn more is important because it helps you accumulate wealth fast. To be able to increase your earning ability you must do the following:

- improve your communication skills
- enhance your credentials
- develop your expertise
- be knowledgeable and skillful
- constantly invest in yourself
- be indispensable
- work hard to improve your visibility

With all these qualities and attributes, you will have a better chance to increase your earning ability. You are now building your human capital and turning it into a veritable profit engine.

Key Takeaways

Think about the things you will take away from strategy 7 and how and when you will implement them.

Topic	Takeaways	Implementation
Reasons for Failure to Increase Earning Ability		
Ways to Increase Earning Ability		

Chapter 10

The Wealth Blueprint

I know money isn't everything, but it certainly is something.

Thisuri Wanniarachchi

This chapter presents the Wealth Blueprint (WB) that I mentioned earlier. The objective of the WB is to determine your financial health. Knowing your financial health is important, because it prepares you to take necessary actions, especially when your financial health is not good, as it can ruin your personal health.

There are eight questions in the WB. Right now, answer all the questions with all honesty.

The Wealth Blueprint

	Questions	Yes	No	If No, Why?
1	Did you pay yourself 10 percent of your salary every month?			
2	Do you stick to your shopping list when you go shopping?			
3	Do you always avoid using credit cards for your purchases?			
4	Do you pay your credit card in full every month?			
5	Do you regularly put aside 5 to 10 percent of your money for high risk investments?			
6	Do you have other sources of income besides your salary?			
7	Do you have trouble paying your bills every month?			
8	Are you feeling stressful because of not having enough money?			

If you answer no to six out of eight questions, you are in serious financial trouble. You need to change the way you handle your financial matters immediately to create your wealth. Ask yourself how much you want to save by the end of the year.

If you want to achieve your financial goals, you must make a commitment to do the following:

- Immediately start paying yourself at least 10 percent every month out of your gross salary. As I have said, this account should not be touched or disturbed. This 10 percent should be in an investment account, earning you at least 7 percent in annual interest, making your money work for you even when you are asleep.

- Stop spending unnecessarily. You must stick to your shopping list. I imagine you have experienced wanting to buy only a few items based on your mental list but buying a lot more. Unfortunately, we can't depend solely on our mental list, as we can easily get distracted when we see things on display, especially during sales or festive seasons. To avoid buying beyond your mental list, have a written list, which you can cross off as you get each item listed. This will help you avoid buying something you don't need. It will also help you save money that you can invest to create your wealth.

- Avoid using credit cards unless you can pay the full balance at the end of the month. Did you know that banks charge interest daily on unpaid balances? They are ripping you off! They have not issued you a credit card but a suicide card. And you die slowly. To avoid being killed by credit cards, don't use them. Better still, don't own one, especially if you can't control yourself. If you still need to have a credit card, leave it at home when you go shopping. Without credit cards and with only money in your pocket, you can control your spending.

- Don't depend on one source of income. Always remember you may be laid off from your current job. The loss of your job could destroy what you and your family once knew and send you into a financial tailspin, particularly if you are the sole earner. Just one short layoff situation has sent many households into deep financial trouble, because the majority of us are living from paycheck to paycheck every month. We also always need to be prepared for when things happen, such as illness, death, accidents, lawsuits, fire, or even vandalism.

The Reality of Life

The stark reality of life for most people is that no matter how well they think they are doing, they are living from paycheck to paycheck. Just one crisis can cause financial problems. Therefore, it is important that you have plans B and C and even D in place should something happen and your current income can't dig you out of the hole.

Normally, those who are financially unprepared face serious financial problems when things hit them suddenly—so always be prepared. Remember, most of us are not living just for the sake of breathing the free air; we want more out of life.

Of course, not all good things cost money, but many valuable experiences and better things are not free either. This is a fact of modern life. Even when your expenses are being met, if you suffer a lack of discretionary income, you may become frustrated and perhaps wonder what you are working for if you can't enjoy hobbies or vacations or other things that are important to you and your family. After all, we should be able to enjoy ourselves from time to time, though not to the point where it jeopardizes our financial stability.

Even when you truly enjoy your career, there should be things outside it that you enjoy at least every now and then, if not on a regular basis. And imagine working for decades and never taking a vacation or doing some of the things you enjoy. When was your last overseas vacation? Perhaps you have never had one, which is the reality for a large number of people. Starting now, you must have another source of income.

Four Ways to Earn Extra Income

You can earn extra cash without quitting your day job and become less dependent on one source of income. Here are four ways:

- **Start your own small business**. It doesn't have to be anything large, fancy, or complicated. You likely won't need expensive facilities, such as office or warehouse space. You can start from home. The point is, where there is a will, there is a way. I have conducted my own training and consulting practices from home for the past eleven years. I've never had a fancy office, but I make sure I deliver professional services that my clients want.

- **Capitalize on your talents or skills**. Use the skills or talents that you already have to create a side business. Many people enjoy writing or are good at creating things with their hands, such as woodwork, jewelry, or art. All these things can be turned into a second income source, depending on the skill and perseverance of the individual. Some people have taken the skills they learned on their job into their own business; they control their hours and work environment as freelancers, landscapers, contractors, salespeople, and consultants, to name a few.

- **Be willing to change.** Get out of your comfort zone, and think outside the box. Never be complacent with what you have. If you think a professional qualification or a postgraduate degree will help you secure a better job and give you a second source of income, go for it. Many of my friends have a passion for photography, and I have encouraged them to take photography courses, even online. They have earned extra money as freelance photographers. The question is, are you willing to change and step out of your comfort zone?

    Hiring ourselves requires a desire for change and a willingness to try something new. Once even small paychecks come in, you will feel validated in your efforts and skills, and you will know for a fact that you can earn more with your own effort and creativity. This will build your confidence, because you will have proof that you are doing a good thing for yourself independently.

Many people involve their entire family in their business. This is often a good route to go down as long as the individuals' age and abilities are taken into consideration and their duties are clearly communicated to them.

When I started my career in public speaking sixteen years ago, I gave motivational talks for free. Because of my passion, I talked to school children, adults, and whoever wanted to listen. I would talk to anyone, from one to a thousand people at a time. By giving free talks, I not only had fun, I got free publicity as well. From then on, the word spread, and I received invitations not only for motivational talks but also for consulting work.

- **Sell the stuff you don't need.** Many people spend nearly all they earn on stuff to fulfill their wants. If you don't plan your spending and just keep fulfilling your wants, any income you have will be gone without you knowing where it went. Look around your home. Do you see things you don't need? You can sell these to get back some money.

  People who increase their income are prone to increasing their spending on wants rather than needs. Stay out for this trap. Track everything you spend for just a month, and see what happens. You will likely see areas in which you can cut back or eliminate spending altogether. If you don't have any extras and are still feeling the squeeze, you need to figure out something you can eliminate from your spending list. Only you can be honest with yourself, as it is you who must pay in the short and long term.

  If you are not interested in or able to increase your income, consider reducing your living expenses. Remember, extras and wants are simply things that are not necessities; they are things you want rather than need.

Extras can often get in the way of your future financial stability, because part or all the money to buy them could be used for your golden years or for large expenditures such as university fees, medical care, or a down payment on a home.

Only you can make the choice. Therefore, choose wisely for your future's sake, and be financially free. Bear in mind that all of us have the potential to be rich. And all that you need is proper planning, effective strategies, inspiration, and a lot of hard work. I believe you can be the next millionaire!

Summary

Checking your Wealth Blueprint is important because it helps to determine your financial health. Once you are aware of your financial health, you must take corrective action. It is hard to pay yourself 10 percent every month if you have never done it before. And it is hard living beneath your means if you have not done it. But try living with a mountain of debts. How do you feel? Whether you like it or not, you must start saving now. And to see the value of your savings, you have to have a strong orientation toward the future. That means doing a little less in the present so that you can create your wealth for the future.

Key Takeaways

Think about the things you will take away from chapter 10 and how and when you will implement them.

Topic	Takeaways	Implementation
Your Wealth Blueprint		
Your Commitment to Achieve Your Financial Goals		
What Are Your Extras?		
What Are Your Wants?		
Ways to Earn Extra Income		

Chapter 11

The Power of Investing

How many millionaires do you know who have become
wealthy by investing in savings accounts? I rest my case.
Robert G. Allen

Never underestimate the power of investing, because the greatest potential for making money is in investment. In fact, investing is the Holy Grail of becoming wealthy, and you should make more money from your investments than from your work. Because of the power of investing, you don't have to own a business to become wealthy. I am not against business ownership, but I believe even as an employee you can become wealthy if you have a strong desire and follow the correct strategies, such as the ones I share in this book.

Unfortunately, many employees are still poor, despite having a good salary. There are many reasons they remain poor. One is that they spend too much and live beyond their means. The other is that they don't invest.

In this chapter, I will discuss some of the reasons most employees don't invest. I will also share some thoughts on why you should invest. I hope you will take the responsibility to invest your money wisely so that financial health is there when you need it one day.

The power of investing vs. the consequences of spending

The Definition of Investing

Let's get started by clearly understand what is meant by *investing*. Investing is the act of using money to buy financial products with the hope that they will appreciate, or grow in value, after you buy them. If the product you bought does increase in its value, you can sell it for a profit. Some investments, such as unit trusts, are meant to be held for a long time before you can realize profitable returns. Other investments, such as shares or stocks, are short term; you can hold them for a year or less and then sell them.

As an **investor**, you become the lending party. The money you invested goes toward a "borrower" who will make use of it and pay back a **return**, much like the principal and interest installment that a debtor has to repay if he or she takes out a loan. The borrower may be a business entity, such as a financial institution or a for-profit company.

Why Employees Don't Invest

Research shows that there are several reasons why few employees invest. The first is that most employees don't believe they can be rich. In their mind, they undervalue themselves and are convinced that they will never become rich. They give the excuse that they are just ordinary employees. Even if they have dreams to be rich, they do nothing about it. Indeed, they never do anything to change their lives and become stuck in poverty. Few of them like the idea of investing, because they believe they might lose money. If they do invest, their mind-set leads them to make certain bad decisions by which they do eventually lose money.

Poor Employees

Unlike rich employees, poor employees undervalue themselves and think small. They become satisfied living in their small mind-set and therefore never taste wealth. Even when they are given the opportunity, they focus only on the obstacles, because their vision is so restricted. They believe that there is nothing for them—so it's not worth trying (see diagram below). In addition, poor employees always try to fit in and avoid being different.

Poor Employee's View

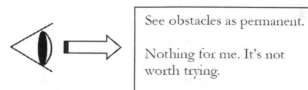

Rich Employees

Unlike poor employees, rich employees always try to be different, focusing on opportunities and setting their own standards. They see obstacles and problems as temporary and always focus on finding solutions. They believe they deserve to have wealth and a good life. Most importantly, they feel they deserve success (see diagram on page 122).

Rich Employee's View

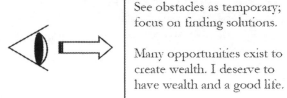

See obstacles as temporary; focus on finding solutions.

Many opportunities exist to create wealth. I deserve to have wealth and a good life.

The second reason most employees don't invest is because they don't realize the potential returns from investment. This could be due to their lack of knowledge about investing. Allow me to ask questions: How many people understand the difference between compound interest and simple interest? Why have so many people deposited their hard-earned cash in savings accounts? Because most people don't understand the power and benefits of compound interest.

Compound interest allows you to earn interest on your interest. With simple interest, you don't; your interest payments stay constant, at a fixed percentage of the original principal. Let's see the difference. Assume you start with a one-off investment of $24,000 at an annual interest rate of 8 percent for twenty years. In the table below, you see that the return you will get from your savings with simple interest will be $62,400 at the end of twenty years. On the other hand, the return that you will get from compound interest will be $111,863 after twenty years. Can you see the big difference?

Starting Principal	$24,000.00
Years	20
Annual Interest Rate	8 percent
Simple Interest	**$62,400.00**
Compound Interest	**$111,863.00**

You can also see from the graph below that investment with compound interest allows for exponential growth, while simple interest provides linear growth. Once people understand the power of compound interest, they view investing differently.

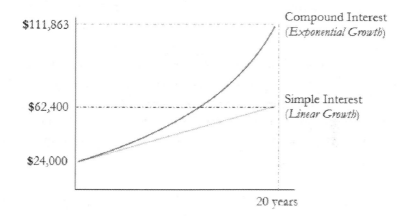

The third reason most employees don't invest is because they have a short-term outlook. They look through a magnifying glass rather than through binoculars, so their vision is narrow. More to the point, they desire immediate gratification. When they get their salary, they want to spend it on something they always wanted. They believe they deserve a treat after working so hard all this while. Is this familiar to you?

In fact, this belief has become epidemic among the poor and middle class. They are always looking forward to immediate gratification. Robert Kiyosaki wrote in his book *Rich Dad Poor Dad*, "Poor people buy luxuries first, while rich people buy luxuries last." This can be seen among so many poor and middle class employees, who are willing to be in debt just to fulfill their immediate desires.

One thing poor and middle-class employees need is to learn from successful people how to view the long-term consequences of their actions. Successful people are always in control of their habits and attitudes when it comes to investment, and they never allow their ego to take control. Successful people know that what they plant today, they will harvest later. They delay their wants because they know they will enjoy them later.

The fourth reason some employees don't invest is that most of them think they don't have enough money to invest. But I don't believe it, as some of my non-investing friends are well paid. I believe that everyone has enough money to start investing, as long as he or she makes it a priority. Unfortunately, most people don't make investing a priority.

If investing is not a priority for you, allow me to ask you a few questions. If you can't find the money to invest now, how can you ever afford to retire? Or send your children to college? How will you be able pay your medical bills when you are no longer covered by your employer? The problem is not insufficient money; it is wasting money every month on something you don't need.

To have surplus money for investment, you must eliminate unnecessary expenses from your household budget. Look at the things you spent money on last month. You may be surprised to find out that some of the things you bought were to fulfill your wants rather than needs. By eliminating unnecessary expenses, you will be able to find "extra" money and convert those dollars into investments. Try it! It is worth it.

You must now shift focus from spending to investing. Think like rich people—they don't spend money unnecessarily; they invest. Remember this: investing can be more productive than business. And by constantly investing, you can create substantial wealth.

Why You Should Invest

As I mentioned earlier, investing is the Holy Grail to becoming a millionaire. Following are the reasons why you should invest.

First, invest to maintain the spending power of your money to counteract inflation. Inflation is defined as a general increase in prices and a fall in the purchasing value of money. It is measured as an annual percentage. As inflation rises, every dollar you own buys a smaller percentage of a good or service. Because of the effects of inflation, you need to grow your savings by at least the rate of inflation. Every year you can see that the costs of goods increase, and this reduces the spending power of your money. The only way to offset this is by growing your money by allowing it to earn interest and then reinvesting it. By doing so, you maintain the spending power of your money.

The second reason you should invest is so your money works for you. This is very important, because you probably don't want to work your entire life. If you do, no employer wants to employ you when you are seventy or eighty. So to ensure a steady flow of income during your golden years, invest; this will secure your future.

Don't wait until you are about to retire to start investing. The sooner the better, because you want your money to work for you as soon as possible. Remember, you can earn money in two ways: by working or by having money work for you. So, don't keep your money under a pillow, where it doesn't work for you.

You will never have more money than what you have. When you invest your money, it generates more either by earning interest or through the buying and selling of assets that increase in their value over time.

The third reason you should invest is because you want to be financially independent. Now is the time to plan for your retirement. Don't expect to depend on the government or your children for support. Always remember that it is not wise to rely on others. Therefore, it makes perfect sense to build your own nest egg while you can and to take care of your own financial health. Nobody will respect you if you become a beggar; to avoid becoming one, you need to build yourself up while you still can. Don't wait until it's too late.

The fourth reason you should invest is to provide strong financial foundations for your children. It was very difficult to build my financial security from scratch, because my parents couldn't afford to provide a firm financial footing for me and for my siblings; they were very poor. Remember that our children's lives in the years to come might be difficult compared to ours now. So any help they can get from their parents is an advantage to them. By taking a positive long-term approach through investing, parents can help to provide a firm financial footing for their children.

Summary

To be wealthy, you must invest and get your money to work for you. Tell yourself that it is never cool to be poor. I have been poor, and it is terrible. You must eliminate all ideas that being poor is acceptable. Remember what Bill Gates said: "If you are born poor, it is not your mistake. But if you die poor, it is your mistake." Also make it a rule that you will never borrow or use debt that won't make money for you. Always remember, to be wealthy you must make it a priority; invest your money rather than spending your money on unnecessary wants.

Good luck with your investments. I am confident I will see you at the top.

Key Takeaways

Think about the things you will take away from chapter 11 and how and when you will implement them.

Topic	Takeaways	Implementation
Why Employees Don't Invest		
Simple Interest		
Compound Interest		
Why You Should Invest		

Appendix A

The Fifty-Two-Week Money Challenge

If saving 10 percent from your salary is a big burden for you (though you should never consider it a burden), try this fifty-two-week money challenge. By taking the challenge, you will successfully save $13,780 in fifty-two weeks.

This challenge is affordable. It gets you started with small amounts that will balloon toward the end of the fifty-two weeks. In fact, I consider this challenge to be one of the simplest ways to save a reasonable amount of money in a year. That money can become the seed money for building your wealth.

Here's how it works. In this challenge, basically you just add a zero to each week. For instance, in week 1, you will add zero to number 1, so the total amount you deposit in your investment account is $10. And in week 2, you will deposit $20, making your total deposit $30. You can see how fast you accumulate the amount by constantly saving every week. In week fifty-two, you will deposit $520, and the total amount you have saved will be $13,780. If you do not do this weekly, you might never save any money for a whole year. And there are many employees out there who do just that.

Now ask yourself how you would feel seeing a total of $13,780 in an investment account that will earn you 7 to 8 percent interest annually? Would you feel great? I would feel great, because I would know I had money for rainy days.

Indeed, the fifty-two-week money challenge is easy. You will become more motivated when you see the total amount you saved over fifty-two weeks. Do this every year, and you will be astonished by the amount of money you save for your future.

Remember, while money doesn't grow on trees, it can definitely grow when you save and invest it wisely. Knowing how to secure your financial well-being is one of the most important things you can do to make your life worth living.

Studies show that you don't have to be a genius when it comes to saving money. All you need is to know what to do, to have a plan, and to stick to your plan. Don't deviate from it! No matter how much or little money you have, if you want to start building your wealth, you have to start saving and investing your money.

The Fifty-Two-Week Money Challenge Table

Week	Deposit ($)	Total ($)	Week	Deposit ($)	Total ($)
1	10	10	27	270	3,780
2	20	30	28	280	4,060
3	30	60	29	290	4,350
4	40	100	30	300	4,650
5	50	150	31	310	4,960
6	60	210	32	320	5,280
7	70	280	33	330	5,610
8	80	360	34	340	5,950
9	90	450	35	350	6,300
10	100	550	36	360	6,660
11	110	660	37	370	7,030
12	120	780	38	380	7,410
13	130	910	39	390	7,800
14	140	1,050	40	400	8,200
15	150	1,200	41	410	8,610
16	160	1,360	42	420	9,030
17	170	1,530	43	430	9,460
18	180	1,710	44	440	9,900
19	190	1,900	45	450	10,350
20	200	2,100	46	460	10,810
21	210	2,310	47	470	11,280
22	220	2,530	48	480	11,760
23	230	2,760	49	490	12,250
24	240	3,000	50	500	12,750
25	250	3,250	51	510	13,260
26	260	3,510	52	520	13,780

Below is a sheet you can use for your fifty-two-week money challenge. You can start with a small amount—for example, in week 1, you deposit $1; in week 2, you deposit $2; and so on. Or you can be more adventurous and deposit bigger amounts. For instance, in week 1 you deposit $100, in week 2 you deposit $200, and by week fifty-two you deposit $5,200. The amount you choose depends on your financial capability. What is most important? That you start saving now.

The Fifty-Two-Week Money Challenge

Week	Deposit ($)	Total ($)	Week	Deposit ($)	Total ($)
1			27		
2			28		
3			29		
4			30		
5			31		
6			32		
7			33		
8			34		
9			35		
10			36		
11			37		
12			38		
13			39		
14			40		
15			41		
16			42		
17			43		
18			44		
19			45		
20			46		
21			47		
22			48		
23			49		
24			50		
25			51		
26			52		

Appendix B
Types of Investment

Bonds. These are grouped under the general category of fixed-income securities. The term *bond* commonly refers to any securities that are founded on debt. When you purchase a bond, you are lending out your money to a company or government. In return, they agree to give you interest on your money and eventually pay you back the amount you lent out. The main attraction of bonds is their relative safety. If you are buying bonds from a stable government, your investment is virtually guaranteed, or risk-free. But the safety and stability come at a cost. Because there is little risk, there is little return. As a result, the rate of return on bonds is lower than that of other securities.

Shares (stocks). When you buy a share, you are buying a small part of a company. If that company makes money, you may be paid a share of the profit, called a dividend. Over time, the price of shares might go up, and you will benefit in terms of a capital gain when you sell your shares. Compared to bonds, shares provide relatively high potential returns. Of course, there is a price for these high potential returns: you risk losing some or all of your investment.

Mutual fund. This is a collection of bonds and stocks. It is a type of investment fund where you pool your money with a number of different investors, which enables you to pay a professional manager who selects certain securities for you.

Certificate of deposit. This is one of the most common investment types, and it works as a savings account, although it has some differences. Just like the way a savings account operates, you receive some interest on your deposit amount at regular intervals.

Exchange traded funds. This is a single investment vehicle that is made up of a group of stocks that represents a certain index. The index is usually a group of some stocks that represent an industry, a sector of an economy, or a certain part of the world.

Money market accounts. These work as a combination of a checking account and a saving account. The money markets pay higher than the traditional types of savings account. The bank usually invests your money on a short-term basis, just like corporate bonds.

Commodities (including gold). These investments don't pay interest or dividends, but they do increase and decrease in value, which can result in a capital gain. The value of commodities often moves in the opposite direction to other asset classes (for example, when share prices go down, gold often increases in value, and vice versa), so investors sometimes buy them to try to protect their money.

Currency (foreign exchange). As well as being used to buy goods and services, foreign currency is also used as an investment. Currency investors look for higher interest rates overseas or hope exchange rates will move in their favor, resulting in a capital gain. Investors, including managed funds, may also use currency to protect, or hedge, other investments overseas.

Derivatives (including options and futures). Derivatives are generally used only by more sophisticated investors, such as managed funds. This can be a confusing and complex area of investing. However, derivatives are built on a fairly simple concept: allowing people to protect themselves, or hedge, against future price movements. For example, a farmer can fix the price today for the milk he will supply in the future. At the same time, a supermarket owner can fix the price now for the milk she will receive in the future.

Unit trust. A unit trust fund consists of a pool of funds collected from a group of investors. This collective investment fund is managed full time by professional fund managers. An investment portfolio typically includes equities, bonds, and assets. A unit trust is a three-way relationship among the manager, the trustee, and the unit holder.

The manager manages and operates the unit trust fund, the trustee holds all the assets, and the unit holder is the investor. The success of a unit trust depends on the expertise and experience of the management company.

Appendix C
The Million-Dollar Challenge

This is my challenge for you: make it to the million-dollar mark. This challenge starts with a base capital of one cent. This will show how far you go and how much you can achieve financially, based on your creativity, persistence, hard work, and determination.

What You Need to Do

First, you need to find one cent. This one cent can be from a friend, your living-room floor, your piggy bank, or a street. How you get your one cent is up to you. When you have secured your cent, what you need to do next is double it to make two cents.

Note: You are not allowed to find another cent, but you must double your cent to make it two cents. For instance, buy something for one cent, and sell it for two cents. How you double your one cent into two cents is up to you.

Then with your two cents, you next challenge is to double that to make four cents, and so on. On the following page are the different levels of the challenge and the financial achievements (amount) as you double your money from one level to the next.

Day/ Week/ Month/ Year	Level	Amount	Level Achieved	Strategy Used	Remarks
	1	1 cent			
	2	2 cents			
	3	4 cents			
	4	8 cents			
	5	16 cents			
	6	32 cents			
	7	64 cents			
	8	$1.28			
	9	$2.56			
	10	$5.12			
	11	$10.24			
	12	$20.48			
	13	$40.96			
	14	$81.92			
	15	$163.84			
	16	$327.68			
	17	$655.36			
	18	$1,310.72			
	19	$2,621.44			
	20	$5,242.88			
	21	$10,485.76			
	22	$20,971.52			
	23	$41,943.04			
	24	$83,886.08			
	25	$167,772.16			
	26	$335,544.32			
	27	$671,088.64			
	28	$1,342,177.28			

As you can see, the table above has the following columns:

- **Day/Week/Month/Year.** This is where you will record the date when you completed each level.

- **Level.** This is the level of the challenge and its corresponding financial amount at various levels.
- **Amount.** This is the amount of money that you expect to earn at different levels of the challenge (by doubling your money).
- **Level Achieved**. This indicates the different levels and the highest level that you can achieve in this challenge.
- **Strategy Used.** This is where you record the strategy (or strategies) you used to get to a different level in this challenge.
- **Remarks.** This is where you record your remarks, including challenges, obstacles, feelings, etc., that you encountered while taking on this challenge.

Here are my questions for you to answer after you'd made some progress in this challenge:

1. Until which level did you find it easy to accomplish the task, and why? _____
2. What is the most difficult task/activity you faced in doing this challenge? _____
3. What deterred you from going beyond the level that you achieved/stopped at? _____
4. What will it takes on your part to reach level 28 of this challenge? _____
5. Do you honestly believe you will be able to achieve level 28, and why? _____
6. What have you learned from taking this challenge?
   _____

Note: It doesn't matter when you achieve your $1 million in this challenge. What matters is that you double your money at every level. In doing so, you need to think strategically, and you need to think out of the box. You will face many challenges and difficulties, but you will find ways to overcome them. Dr. Norman Vincent Peale said in his book *The Power of Positive Thinking*, "Believe in yourself. Have faith in your abilities."

Most importantly, if you have made some money, you must control your urge to spend it. Your objective is to double your money so that you can achieve your goal in this challenge—that is, to make a million dollars. Good luck with this challenge!

References

Bandura, Albert. 1986. *Social Foundations of Thought and Action.* Englewood Cliffs, NJ: Prentice-Hall.

Clason, George. 1955. *The Richest Man in Babylon—The Success Secrets of the Ancients.* New York: Penguin.

Conwell, Russell. 2008. *Acres of Diamonds.* New York: Penguin.

Godin, Seth. 2011. *Linchpin: Are You Indispensable?* New York: Penguin.

Hill, Napoleon. 1953. *Think and Grow Rich.* Cleveland, OH: The Ralston Publishing.

Kiong, Frank. 2010. *Dare to Change: A Step-By-Step Guide for Top Achievers.* Sarawak, Malaysia: Infographic Press.

Kiyosaki, Robert. 2011. *Rich Dad Poor Dad.* Scottsdale, AZ: Plata Publishing.

Peale, Norman V. 1996. *The Power of Positive Thinking.* New York: Random House.

Riley, Pat. 1993. *The Winner Within: A Life Plan for Team Players.* New York: Berkley Trade.

Templar, Richard. 2012. *The Rules of Wealth.* Upper Saddle River, NJ: FT Press.

Tracy, Brian. 2012. *The Power of Self-Confidence: Become Unstoppable, Irresistible, and Unafraid in Every Area of Your Life.* Somerset, NJ: Wiley.

About the Author

DR. FRANK KIONG is a professional trainer, author, business, and wealth-building coach. He was a university director and business professor who taught finance, investment, marketing, leadership, portfolio management, entrepreneurship, research methods, strategic management, and international business. Dr. Kiong is also the author of motivational books *Dare to Change: A Step-by-Step Guide for Top Achievers* and *Peeling Your Onion: The Magic to Your True Potential*.

As a professional trainer and highly sought-after business and motivational speaker, Dr. Kiong has conducted and facilitated numerous motivational, business, leadership, and financial workshops and seminars, both domestically and internationally.

He holds a PhD in business management from the University of Stirling in Scotland, a specialized master's degree in finance, and a bachelor's degree in finance from Saint Louis University in St. Louis, Missouri.

Printed in the United States
By Bookmasters